To Carmen Sheldon,
my comrade in Design,
my friend in Life.
— with great love,
R.

More matter is being printed and published today than ever before, and every publisher of an advertisement, pamphlet, or book expects his material to be read. Publishers and, even more so, readers want what is important to be clearly laid out. They will not read anything that is troublesome to read, but are pleased with what looks clear and well arranged, for it will make their task of understanding easier. For this reason, the important part must stand out and the unimportant must be subdued . . . .

The technique of modern typography must also adapt itself to the speed of our times. Today, we cannot spend as much time on a letter heading or other piece of jobbing as was possible even in the nineties.

—*Jan Tschichold, 1935*

Contents

Design principles

The Joshua tree epiphany — 11

Proximity
Alignment
Repetition
Contrast

Proximity — 15

The basic purpose
How to get it
What to avoid

Alignment — 31

The basic purpose
How to get it
What to avoid

Repetition — 49

The basic purpose
How to get it
What to avoid

Contrast — 63

The basic purpose
How to get it
What to avoid

Review 79

Extra tips & tricks 87

THE

Non-

Designer's

Design

Book

SECOND EDITION

**design
and
typographic
principles
for the
visual
novice**

Robin Williams

Peachpit Press
Berkeley
California

The Non-Designer's Design Book
second edition
ROBIN WILLIAMS

©2004 by Robin Williams

Peachpit Press
1249 Eighth Street
Berkeley, California 94710
800.283.9444
510.524.2178
510.524.2221 FAX

Editor:	Nancy Davis
Cover design and production:	John Tollett
Interior design:	Robin Williams
Production:	Laura Taylor and Robin Williams

Peachpit Press is a division of Pearson Education.
Find us on the web at www.peachpit.com.

The quote by Jan White on page 165 is from the out-of-print book *How to Spec Type*, by Alex White. Reprinted courtesy of Roundtable Press, Inc. Copyright 1987 by Roundtable Press, Inc.

The charming pen-and-ink drawing of the wicket woof on pages 44 and 45 are by Jon Vlakos, reprinted courtesy of Swamp Press. Copyright 1990 by Swamp Press. You can order an exquisite little handmade letterpressed booklet of the tale of "Ladle Rat Rotten Hut," by Howard L. Chace. Send $4 per booklet, plus $2.50 per order to Swamp Press, 323 Pelham Road, Amherst, MA, 01002.

The portions of other stories, such as "Guilty Looks Enter Tree Beers," "Center Alley," and "Violate Huskings" are from a long out-of-print book by Howard L. Chace called *Anguish Languish*. It is our understanding that these delightful stories are now in the public domain. They are easily found on the Internet.

ISBN: 0-321-19385-7

10 9 8 7 6 5 4 3 2 1

Printed and bound in the United States of America

Designing with Type

EXTRAS

But, is it appropriate?
—*Edward Gottschall*

It stinks.
—*Herb Lubalin*

Is this book for you?

This book is written for all the people who need to design pages, but have no background or formal training in design. I don't mean just those who are designing fancy packaging or lengthy brochures—I mean the secretaries whose bosses now tell them to design the newsletters, church volunteers who are putting out information to their congregations, small business owners who are creating their own advertising, students who understand that a better-looking paper often means a better grade, professionals who realize that an attractive presentation garners greater respect, teachers who have learned that students respond more positively to information that is well laid out, statisticians who see that numbers and stats can be arranged in a way that invites reading rather than sleeping, and on and on.

This book assumes you don't have the time or interest to study design and typography, but you would like to know how to make your pages look better. Well, the premise of this book is age-old: knowledge is power. Most people can look at a poorly designed page and state that they don't like it, but they don't know what to do to fix it. In this book I will point out four basic concepts that are used in virtually every well-designed job. These concepts are clear and concrete. If you don't know what's wrong with it, how can you fix it? Once you recognize the concepts, you will notice whether or not they have been applied to your pages. *Once you can name the problem, you can find the solution.*

This book is not intended to take the place of four years of design school. I do not pretend you will automatically become a brilliant designer after you read this little book. But I do guarantee you will never again look at a page in the same way. I guarantee if you follow these basic principles, your work will look more professional, organized, unified, and interesting. And *you* will feel empowered.

With a smile, *Robin*

Mini-glossary

The **baseline** is the invisible line on which type sits (see page 142).

Body copy, body text, and sometimes just plain **body** or **text** refer to the main block of text that you read, as opposed to headlines, subheads, titles, etc. Body text is usually between 9 and 12 point type.

A **bullet** is a little marker, typically used in a list instead of numbers, or between words. This is the standard bullet: • .

A **dingbat** is a small, ornamental character, like this: ■ ❖ ✓ ✍ ❤. You might have the fonts Zapf Dingbats or Wingdings, which are made up of dingbats.

Elements are the separate objects on the page. An element might be a single line of text, or a graphic, or a group of items that are so close together they are perceived as one unit. To know the number of elements on a page, squint your eyes and count the number of times your eye stops, seeing each separate item.

Extended text refers to the body copy (as above) when there is a lot of it, as in a book or a long report.

When I talk of your **eye** or the **eye flow,** I'm referring to your eyes as if they are one independent body. As a designer, you can control the way someone moves her "eye" around a page (the eye flow), so you need to become more conscious of how *your* eye moves around on the page.

Justified type is when a block of text is lined up on both the left and right edges.

A **rule** is a line, a drawn line, such as the one under the headline "Mini-glossary," above.

White space is the space on a page that is not occupied by any text or graphics. You might call it "blank" space. Beginners tend to be afraid of white space; professional designers "use" lots of white space.

Trapped white space is when the white, or blank, space on a page is trapped between elements (such as text or photos), with no space through which to flow.

The Joshua tree epiphany

This short chapter explains the **four basic principles** in general, each of which will be explained in detail in the following chapters. But first I want to tell you a little story that made me realize the importance of being able to name things, since naming these principles is the key to having power over them.

Many years ago I received a tree identification book for Christmas. I was at my parents' home, and after all the gifts had been opened I decided to go out and identify the trees in the neighborhood. Before I went out, I read through part of the book. The first tree in the book was the Joshua tree because it only took two clues to identify it. Now the Joshua tree is a really weird-looking tree and I looked at that picture and said to myself, "Oh, we don't have that kind of tree in Northern California. That is a weird-looking tree. I would know if I saw that tree, and I've never seen one before."

So I took my book and went outside. My parents lived in a cul-de-sac of six homes. Four of those homes had Joshua trees in the front yard. I had lived in that house for thirteen years, and I had never seen a Joshua tree. I took a walk around the block, and there must have been a sale at the nursery when everyone was landscaping their new homes—at least 80 percent of the homes had Joshua trees in the front yards. *And I had never seen one before!* Once I was conscious of the tree—once I could name it—I saw it everywhere. Which is exactly my point: Once you can name something, you're conscious of it. You have power over it. You own it. You're in control.

So now you're going to learn the names of several design principles. And you are going to be in control of your pages.

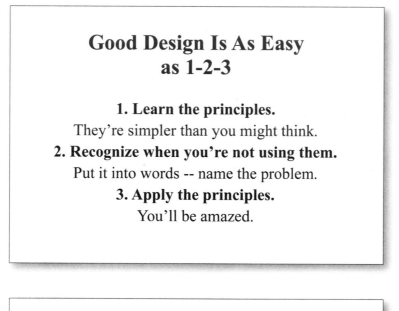

The four basic principles

The following is a brief overview of the basic principles of design that appear in every well-designed piece of work. Although I discuss each one of these principles separately, keep in mind they are really interconnected. Rarely will you apply only one principle.

Contrast

The idea behind contrast is to avoid elements on the page that are merely *similar.* If the elements (type, color, size, line thickness, shape, space, etc.) are not the *same,* then make them **very different.** Contrast is often the most important visual attraction on a page—it's what makes a reader look at the page in the first place.

Repetition

Repeat visual elements of the design throughout the piece. You can repeat colors, shapes, textures, spatial relationships, line thicknesses, fonts, sizes, graphic concepts, etc. This develops the organization and strengthens the unity.

Alignment

Nothing should be placed on the page arbitrarily. Every element should have some visual connection with another element on the page. This creates a clean, sophisticated, fresh look.

Proximity

Items relating to each other should be grouped close together. When several items are in close proximity to each other, they become one visual unit rather than several separate units. This helps organize information, reduces clutter, and gives the reader a clear structure.

Umm . . .

When gathering these four principles from the vast maze of design theory, I thought there must be some appropriate and memorable acronym within these conceptual ideas that would help people remember them. Well, uh, there is a memorable—but rather inappropriate—acronym. Sorry.

Good communication

is as

stimulating

as black coffee...

and just

as hard

to sleep after.

ANNE MORROW LINDBERGH

Proximity

Very often in beginners' designs, the words and phrases and graphics are strung out all over the place, filling corners and taking up lots of room so there won't be any empty space. There seems to be a fear of empty space. When pieces of a design are scattered all over, the page appears unorganized and the information may not be instantly accessible to the reader.

The principle of proximity states that you **group related items together,** move them physically close to each other so the related items are seen as one cohesive group rather than a bunch of unrelated bits.

Items or groups of information that are *not* related to each other should *not* be in close proximity (nearness) to the other elements, which gives the reader an instant visual clue as to the organization and content of the page.

The very simple example below illustrates this concept. In the list on the left, what do you assume about all those flowers? Probably that they have something in common, right? In the list on the right, what do you assume? It appears that the last four flowers are somehow different from the others. You understand this *instantly*. And you understand it without even being conscious of it. You *know* the last four flowers are somehow different *because they are physically separated from the rest of the list.* That's the concept of proximity—on a page (as in life), physical closeness implies a relationship.

My Flower List

Marigold
Pansy
Rue
Woodbine
Daisy
Cowslip
Carnation
Primrose
Violets
Pink

My Flower List

Marigold
Pansy
Rue
Woodbine
Daisy
Cowslip

Carnation
Primrose
Violets
Pink

Take a look at this typical business card layout, below. How many separate elements do you see in that small space? How many times does your eye stop to look at something?

Does your eye stop five times? Of course—there are five separate items on this little card.

Where do you begin reading? In the middle, probably, because that phrase is boldest.

What do you read next— left to right (because you read English)?

What happens when you get to the bottom-right corner, where does your eye go?

Do you wander around making sure you didn't miss any corners?

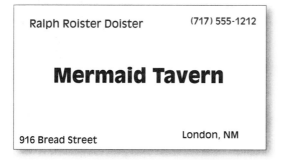

And what if I confuse the issue even further:

Now that there are two bold phrases, where do you begin? Do you start in the upper left? Do you start in the center?

After you read those two items, where do you go? Perhaps you bounce back and forth between the bold words, nervously trying to catch the other words in the corners.

Do you know when you're finished?

Does your friend follow the same pattern you did? No?

When several items are in close proximity to each other, they become *one* visual unit rather than several *separate* units. As in life, **the proximity, or the closeness, implies a relationship.**

By grouping similar elements into one unit, several things instantly happen: The page becomes more organized. You understand where to begin reading the message, and you know when you are finished. And the "white space" (the space around the letters) becomes more organized as well.

A problem with the previous card is that not one of the items on the card seems related to any other item. It is not clear where you should begin reading the card, and it is not clear when you are finished.

If I do one thing to this business card—**if I group related elements together, into closer proximity**—look what happens:

Mermaid Tavern

Ralph Roister Doister

916 Bread Street
London, NM
(717) 555 1212

Is there any question now about where you begin to read the card? Where you go next? Do you know when you're finished?

With that one simple concept, this card is now organized both **intellectually** and **visually.** And thus it communicates more clearly.

Shown below is a typical newsletter masthead. How many separate elements are in this piece? Does any item of information seem related to any other, judging from the placement?

Take a moment to decide which items should be grouped into closer proximity and which should be separated.

The two items on the top left are in close proximity to each other, implying a relationship. But **should** these two have a relationship?

How about the date and the issue information? They should be closer together since they both identify this particular issue.

In the example below, the proper relationships have been established.

Notice I did a couple of other things along the way:

Changed everything from all caps to lowercase, which gave me room to make the title stronger and bolder.

Changed the corners from rounded to straight, giving the piece a cleaner, stronger look.

Enlarged the airplane and let it break out of the boundary, a common graphic trick that opens up the space.

When you create a flyer, a brochure, a newsletter, or whatever, you *know* which pieces of information are logically connected, you know which information should be emphasized, and what can be de-emphasized. Express that information graphically by grouping it.

Media Disks
Children's CDs
Educational CDs
Entertainment CDs
DVDs
Educational
Early learning
Language arts
Science
Math
Teacher Tools
Books
Teacher workbooks
Videos
Hardware &
Accessories
Cables
Input devices
Mass storage
Memory
Modems
Printers & supplies
Video and sound

Media Disks
Children's CDs
Educational CDs
Entertainment CDs
DVDs

Educational
Early learning
Language arts
Science
Math

Teacher Tools
Books
Teacher workbooks
Videos

**Hardware &
Accessories**
Cables
Input devices
Mass storage
Memory
Disk drives
Printers & supplies
Video and sound

Obviously, this list needs some formatting to make it understandable. But the biggest problem with this list is that everything is close to everything else, so there is no way to see the relationships or the organization.

The same list has been formed into visual groups. I'm sure you already do this automatically—I'm just suggesting that you now do it consciously and with more strength.

Notice I added some contrast to the headlines, and repeated that contrast.

Sometimes when grouping like items in close proximity, you need to make some changes, such as in the size or weight or placement of text or graphics. Text does not have to be 12 point! Information that is subsidiary to the main message, such as the volume number and year of a newsletter, can often be as small as 7 or 8 point.

Chamber Concert Series
Egley Junior College

Friday February 8 at 8 p.m.   Alexander String Quartet
Mozart, K387, Bartok#3, Beethoven, Opus 59, #1
Sam Pritchert & Ethel Libitz, violins;
Sandra Yarbrough, viola; Mark Wilson, cello
Friday, March 1, 8 p.m. Trio Artaria
Beethoven "Archduke" Trio, and trios by
Haydn, Schoenberg and Magnard
Richard Samson Norartz, violin
Reception following concert in Egley Art Gallery
Friday, April 26 at 8 p.m. Egley Chamber Players
Brahms G Minor Piano Quartet,
Schubert Sonata
Polly Hollyfield, violin; Linda Batticioli, viola;
Norinne Antiqua-Tempest, cello;
Margaret Park-Raynolds, flute; Robin Plantz, piano
All concerts in Newman Auditorium,
Emeritus Hall, Community Education
Tickets $10 and $8
For ticket information phone 555-1212

Not only is this page visually boring, but it is difficult to find the information—exactly what is going on, where is it happening, what time is it at, etc.

For instance, how many concerts are in the series?

The idea of proximity doesn't mean that *everything* is closer together; it means elements that are *intellectually* connected, that have some sort of communication relationship, should also be *visually* connected. Other separate elements or groups of elements should *not* be in close proximity. The closeness *or* lack of closeness indicates the relationship.

Chamber Concert Series

Alexander String Quartet
Mozart, K387, Bartok#3, Beethoven, Opus 59 #1
Sam Pritchert & Ethel Libitz, violins;
Sandra Yarbrough, viola; Mark Wilson, cello
Friday, February 8, 8 P.M.

Trio Artaria
Beethoven "Archduke" Trio,
and trios by Haydn, Schoenberg and Magnard
Richard Samson Norartz, violin
Friday, March 1, 8 p.m.
　　Reception following concert in Egley Art Gallery

Santa Rosa Chamber Players
Brahms G Minor Piano Quartet, Schubert Sonata
Polly Hollyfield, violin; Linda Batticioli, viola;
Norinne Antiqua-Tempest, cello;
Margaret Park-Raynolds, flute; Robin Plantz, piano
Friday, April 26, 8 p m

Egley Junior College
All concerts in Newman Auditorium, Emeritus Hall
Community Education
Tickets $10 and $8
For ticket information phone 555.1212

How many concerts are in the series?

First I intellectually grouped the information together (in my head or sketched onto paper), then physically set the text in groups on the page. Notice the spacing between the three performances is the same, indicating that these three groups are somehow related.

The subsidiary information is farther away—you instantly know it is not one of the performances.

Below you see the same example as on the previous page. Glance at it quickly—now what do you assume about the three concerts?

And why exactly do you assume one concert is different from the others? Because one is *separate* from the others. You *instantly* know that concert is somehow different because of the spatial relationships.

Chamber Concert Series

Alexander String Quartet
Mozart, K387, Bartok#3, Beethoven, Opus 59 #1
Sam Pritchert & Ethel Libitz, violins;
Sandra Yarbrough, viola; Mark Wilson, cello
Friday, February 8, 8 P.M.

Trio Artaria
Beethoven "Archduke" Trio,
and trios by Haydn, Schoenberg and Magnard
Richard Samson Norartz, violin
Friday, March 1, 8 p.m.
   Reception following concert in Egley Art Gallery

Santa Rosa Chamber Players
Brahms G Minor Piano Quartet, Schubert Sonata
Polly Hollyfield, violin; Linda Batticioli, viola;
Norinne Antiqua-Tempest, cello;
Margaret Park-Raynolds, flute; Robin Plantz, piano
Friday, April 26, 8 p.m.

Egley Junior College
All concerts in Newman Auditorium, Emeritus Hall
Community Education
Tickets $10 and $8
For ticket information phone 527.4371

It's really amazing how much information we get from a quick glance at a page. Thus it becomes your responsibility to make sure the reader gets the **correct** *information.*

The designer's intention with this garage sale flyer was probably to create something fun and energetic, but at first glance, can you tell when and where the sale is happening?

Free Coffee!   Free Donuts!

Garage Sale!

Toys

Victorian
Fainting Couch   Vintage Clothing   Large Bird Cage

Good-As-New
Dentistry Tools

25-lb. bags
of bird feed   1950s
Beauty Salon
equipment

1942
Motorola Radio   Large Bird

Proceeds go to
the Mary Sidney
Education Fund   527 Happening Road

. . .and much more!   Saturday 9-3

Garage Sale!
Saturday 9-3   527 Happening Road

Good-As-New
Dentistry Tools

25-lb. bags of
bird feed

Large Bird and
Large Bird Cage

Victorian
Fainting Couch

1950s Beauty Salon
Equipment

1942 Motorola Radio
—still works

Vintage Clothing

Toys

. . . and much more!

Free Coffee and Donuts!
Proceeds go to the Mary Sidney Education Fund

By using the principle of proximity to organize the information, we can communicate immediately who, what, when, and where. No losing potential customers because they give up searching through the vast field of slanted text.

You're probably already using the principle of proximity in your work, but you may not be pushing it as far as you could to make it truly effective. Really look at those pages, at those elements, and see which items should be grouped together.

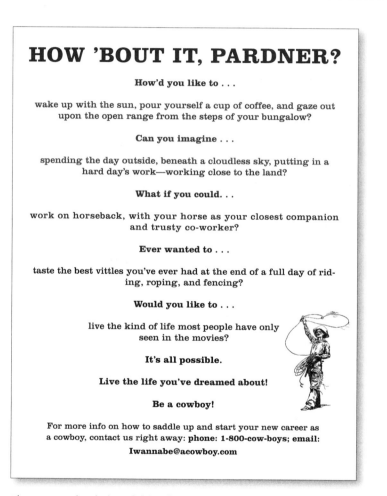

The person who designed this mini-poster typed two Returns after each headline **and** paragraph. Thus the headlines are each the same distance from the body copy above and below, so they appear to be separate, unconnected items. You can't tell if the headline belongs to the text above it or below it because the distances are the same.

There is lots of white space available here, but it's all broken up. And there is white space where it doesn't belong, like between the headlines and their related texts. When white space is "trapped" like this, it tends to visually push the elements apart.

If there are too many separate items, group the ones that have relationships. If there are areas on the page where the organization is not perfectly clear, see if items are in proximity that *shouldn't* be. Use the simple design feature of space to make the page not only more organized, but nicer to look at.

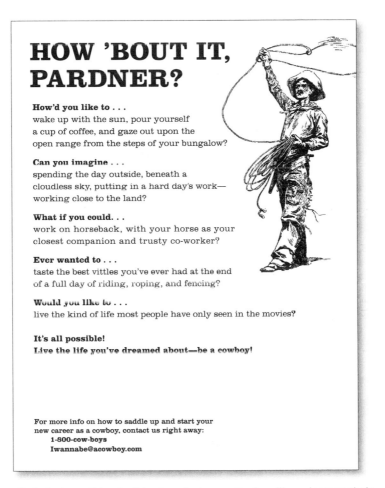

If I do just one thing to this piece, just move the headlines closer to their related paragraphs of text, several things happen:

> The organization is clearer.

> The white space is not trapped within elements.

> There appears to be more room on the page so the mini-poster is not so crowded.

I also put the phone and email address on separate lines—but grouped together and separated—so they'll stand out as important information.

And you probably noticed that I changed the centered alignment to flush left (that's the principle of alignment, as explained in the next chapter), which provided more room for the cowboy graphic.

Proximity is really just a matter of being a little more conscious, of doing what you do naturally, but pushing the concept a little further. Once you become aware of the importance of the relationships between lines of type, you will start noticing its effect. Once you start noticing the effect, you own it, you have power over it, you are in control.

I took this ad right out of the newspaper. Really. One of the biggest problems with it (besides being all caps) is that all the information is one big hunk.

Before trying to design with this information, write out the separate pieces of information that belong together; group the elements. You know how to do this—simply use your brain.

Once you have the groups of information, you can play with them on the page. You have a computer—try lots of options.

Rarely is the principle of proximity the only answer to a problematic page. The other three principles are intrinsic to the design process and you will usually find yourself using all four. But take them one at a time—*start* with proximity. In the example below, I decided which elements should be close together, then experimented with the other principles (and fonts).

Never before in Galaria history...

has one been able to taste 50 Galaria restaurants and 50 internationally acclaimed wineries at one location on one day. Don't miss out! Join us for this big event!

$35 admission includes unlimited tastings, souvenir glass, and entertainment.

A portion of the proceeds will benefit the Galaria Food Brigade, helping us feed our hungry neighbors.

ANNUAL GALARIA WINE & CHILE FIESTA

7th Annual Galaria Wine & Chile Fiesta

Saturday 12 noon to 4:30 P.M. at the El Dorado Hotel

Advance tickets are still available at Galaria News and at our Plaza Americado Box Office. Limited tickets will also be available at the door.

The biggest problem with the original ad is that there is no separation of information. Setting all the text in all caps in one big block also took up all the space, so there was no extra, blank, "white" space to rest your eyes. It's okay to set the type smaller than 12 point! Really!

This is only one of dozens of possibilities for arranging the groups of information. I also used the principles of alignment and contrast, which you will be reading about shortly.

The simple principle of proximity can make web pages easier to navigate by collecting information into logical groups. Check any web site that you feel is easy to get around in—you'll find information grouped into logical clumps.

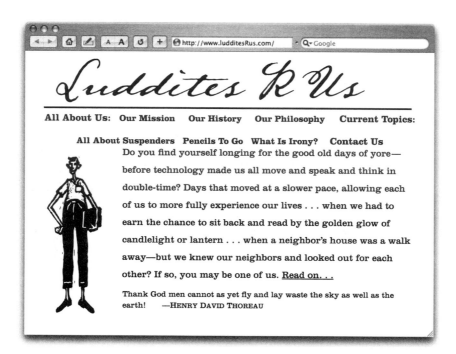

The information on this page is muddled. Look at the site links just under the title. Are they all equal in meaning? They appear to be—but they're not.

I have to repeat myself: Intellectually, you already know how to use proximity. You already know how to collect pieces of information into their appropriate groups. All you need to do is transfer that skill to the printed page.

Luddites R Us

All About Us
  Our Mission
  Our History
  Our Philosophy

Current Topics
All About
  Suspenders
Pencils To Go
What Is Irony?

Contact Us

Do you find yourself longing for the good old days of yore—before technology made us all move and speak and think in double-time? Days that moved at a slower pace, allowing each of us to more fully experience our lives . . . when we had to earn the chance to sit back and read by the golden glow of candlelight or lantern . . . when a neighbor's house was a walk away—but we knew our neighbors and looked out for each other?

If so, you may be one of us. Read on . . .

Thank God men cannot as yet fly and lay waste the sky as well as the earth!
—HENRY DAVID THOREAU

I moved all the site links into one column to show their relationships to one another (and moved the nerd-man to the other side).

I set the quotation further away from the main body copy since it's not directly related.

I also used the principle of alignment (discussed in Chapter 3): I used flush-left alignment and made sure each element lined up with something else.

Summary of proximity

When several items are in close **proximity** to each other, they become one visual unit rather than several separate units. Items relating to each other should be grouped together. Be conscious of where your eye is going: where do you start looking; what path do you follow; where do you end up; after you've read it, where does your eye go next? You should be able to follow a logical progression through the piece, from a definite beginning to a definite end.

The basic purpose

The basic purpose of proximity is to **organize.** Other principles come into play as well, but simply grouping related elements together into closer proximity automatically creates organization. If the information is organized, it is more likely to be read and more likely to be remembered. As a by-product of organizing the communication, you also create more appealing (more organized) *white space* (designers' favorite term).

How to get it

Squint your eyes slightly and **count** the number of visual elements on the page by counting the number of times your eye stops. If there are more than three to five items on the page (of course it depends on the piece), see which of the separate elements can be grouped together into closer proximity to become one visual unit.

What to avoid

Avoid too many separate elements on a page.

Don't stick things in the corners and in the middle.

Avoid leaving equal amounts of white space between elements unless each group is part of a subset.

Avoid even a split second of confusion over whether a headline, subhead, caption, graphic, etc., belongs with its related material. Create a relationship among elements with close proximity.

Don't create relationships with elements that don't belong together! If they are not *related,* move them apart from each other.

Alignment

New designers tend to put text and graphics on the page wherever there happens to be space, often without regard to any other items on the page. What this creates is the slightly-messy-kitchen effect—you know, with a cup here, a plate there, a napkin on the floor, a pot in the sink, a spill on the floor. It doesn't take much to clean up the slightly messy kitchen, just as it doesn't take much to clean up a slighty messy design that has weak alignments.

The principle of alignment states that **nothing should be placed on the page arbitrarily. Every item should have a visual connection with something else on the page**. The principle of alignment forces you to be conscious—no longer can you just throw things on the page wherever there happens to be room.

When items are aligned on the page, it creates a stronger cohesive unit. Even when aligned elements are physically separated from each other, there is an invisible line that connects them, both in your eye and in your mind. Although you might have separated certain elements to indicate their relationships (using the principle of proximity), the principle of alignment is what tells the reader that even though these items are not close, they belong to the same piece. The following pages illustrate this idea.

Take a look at this business card, the same one you saw in the last chapter. Part of its problem is that nothing is aligned with anything else. In this little space, there are elements with three different alignments: flush left, flush right, and centered. The two groups of text in the upper corners are not lined up along the same baseline, nor are they aligned at the left or right edges with the two groups at the bottom of the card (which don't line up along their baselines, either).

The elements on this card look like they were just thrown on and stuck. Not one of the elements has any connection with any other element on the card.

Take a moment to decide which items should be grouped into closer proximity, and which should be separated.

Mermaid Tavern
Ralph Roister Doister

916 Bread Street
London, NM
(717) 555-1212

By moving all the elements over to the right and giving them one alignment, the information is instantly more organized. (Of course, grouping the related elements into closer proximity helped, too.)

The text items now have a common boundary; this boundary connects them together.

In the example (repeated below) that you saw in the proximity section, the text is also aligned—it's aligned down the center. But if text is aligned, instead, on the left or the right, the invisible line that connects the text is much stronger because it has a hard vertical edge to follow. This gives left- and right-aligned text a cleaner and more dramatic look. Compare the two examples below, then we'll talk about it on the following pages.

Mermaid Tavern
Ralph Roister Doister

916 Bread Street
London, NM
(717) 555-1212

This example has a nice arrangement with the text items grouped into logical proximity. The text is center-aligned over itself, and centered on the page. Although this is a legitimate alignment, the edges are "soft"; you don't really see the strength of the line.

Mermaid Tavern
Ralph Roister Doister

916 Bread Street
London, NM
(717) 555-1212

This has the same logical arrangement as above, but it is now right-aligned. Can you see the "hard" edge on the right?

There is a strong invisible line connecting the edges of these two groups of text. You can actually see the edge. **The strength of this edge is what gives strength to the layout.**

The invisible line runs right down here, connecting the text.

Do you tend to automatically center everything? A centered alignment is the most common alignment that beginners use—it's very safe, it feels comfortable. A centered alignment creates a more formal look, a more sedate look, a more ordinary and oftentimes downright dull look. Take notice of the designs you like. I guarantee that most designs that have a sophisticated look are not centered. I know it's difficult, as a beginner, to break away from a centered alignment; you'll have to force yourself to do it at first. But combine a strong flush right or left alignment with good use of proximity and you will be amazed at the change in your work.

Business Plan
for
Red Hen Enterprises

by Shannon Williams
March 20, 2006

Business Plan
for
Red Hen Enterprises

by Shannon Williams
March 20, 2006

This is a typical report cover, yes? This standard format presents a dull, almost amateurish look, which may influence someone's initial reaction to the report.

The strong flush-left alignment gives the report cover a more sophisticated impression. Even though the author's name is far from the title, that invisible line of the strong alignment connects the two text blocks.

Stationery has so many design options! But too often it ends up with a flat, centered alignment. You can be very free with placement on a piece of stationery—but remember alignment.

This isn't bad, but the centered layout is a little dull, and the border closes the space, making it feel confined.

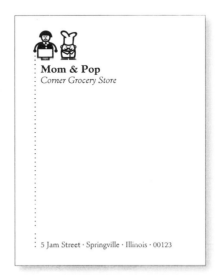

A flush-left alignment makes the page a little more sophisticated. Limiting the dotted line to the left side opens the page and emphasizes the alignment.

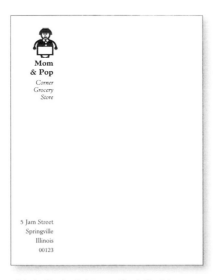

This is flush right, on the left side. I made some changes in the typeface.

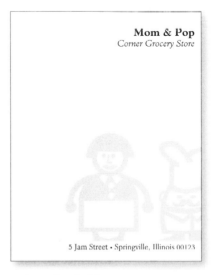

Be brave! Be bold!

I'm not suggesting that you *never* center anything! Just be conscious of the effect a centered alignment has—is that really the look you want to portray? Sometimes it is; for instance, most weddings are rather sedate, formal affairs, so if you want to center your wedding announcement, do so consciously and joyfully.

Centered. Really rather dull.

If you're going to center text, then at least make it obvious!

Experiment with uncentering the block of centered type.

If you're going to center the text, experiment with making it more dramatic in some other way.

Sometimes you can add a bit of a twist on the centered arrangement, such as centering the type, but setting the block of type itself off center. Or set the type high on the page to create more tension. Or set a very casual, fun typeface in a very formal, centered arrangement. What you *don't* want to do is set Times 12-point with double-Returns!

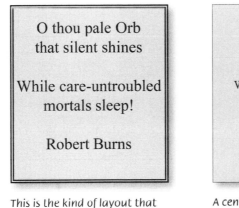

O thou pale Orb
that silent shines

While care-untroubled
mortals sleep!

Robert Burns

This is the kind of layout that gives "centered" a bad name: Boring typeface, type that is too large, crowded text, double Returns, dorky border.

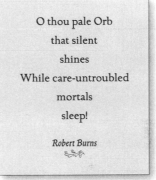

O thou pale Orb

that silent

shines

While care-untroubled

mortals

sleep!

Robert Burns

A centered alignment needs extra care to make it work. This layout uses a classic typeface sized fairly small (relatively), more space between the lines, lots of white space around the text, no border.

O thou pale
Orb
that silent
shines
While care-
untroubled
mortals
sleep!

Emphasize a tall, slender centered layout with a tall, slender piece of paper.

O thou pale Orb
that silent shines
while care-untroubled
mortals sleep!

Robert Burns

Emphasize a wide, centered layout with a wide spread. Try your next flyer sideways.

You're accustomed to working with text alignments. Until you have more training, stick to the guideline of using one text alignment on the page: either all text is flush left, flush right, or centered.

This text is **flush left.**
Some people call it
quad left, or you can say
it is left aligned.

This text is **flush right.**
Some people call it
quad right, or you can
say it is right aligned.

This text is **centered.**
If you are going to
center text,
make it
obvious.

See, in this paragraph it is
difficult to tell if this text
was centered purposely
or perhaps accidentally.
The line lengths are not
the same, but they are not
really different. If you can't
instantly tell that the type
is centered, why bother?

This text is **justified.** Some people call it quad left and right, and some call it blocked—the text lines up on both sides. Whatever you call it, don't do it unless your line length is long enough to avoid awkward gaps   between   the   words.

Occasionally you can get away with using both flush right and flush left text on the same page, but make sure you align them in some way!

Robert Burns

*Poems in Scots
and English*

The most
complete edition
available of
Scotland's
great poet.

In this example, the title and the subtitle are flush left, but the description is centered—there is no common alignment between the two elements of text. They don't have any connection to each other.

Robert Burns

*Poems in Scots
and English*

The most
complete edition
available
of Scotland's
great poet.

Although these two elements still have two different alignments (the top is flush left and the bottom is flush right), the edge of the descriptive text below aligns with the right edge of the title above, connecting the elements with an invisible line. This was not an accident!

When you place other items on the page, make sure each one has some visual alignment with another item on the page. If lines of text are across from each other horizontally, align their baselines. If there are several separate blocks of text, align their left or right edges. If there are graphic elements, align their edges with other edges on the page. Nothing should be placed on the page arbitrarily!

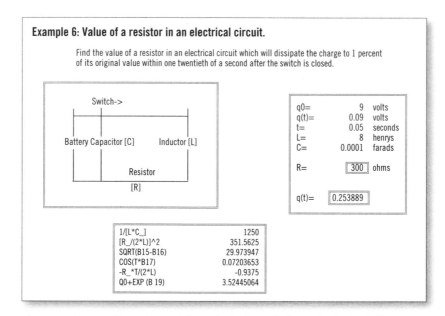

Example 6: Value of a resistor in an electrical circuit.

Find the value of a resistor in an electrical circuit which will dissipate the charge to 1 percent of its original value within one twentieth of a second after the switch is closed.

q0=	9 volts
q(t)=	0.09 volts
t=	0.05 seconds
L=	8 henrys
C=	0.0001 farads
R=	300 ohms
q(t)=	0.253889

Switch->

Battery Capacitor [C]   Inductor [L]

Resistor

[R]

1/[L*C_]	1250
[R_/(2*L)]^2	351.5625
SQRT(B15-B16)	29.973947
COS(T*B17)	0.07203653
-R_*T/(2*L)	-0.9375
Q0+EXP (B 19)	3.52445064

There are two problems here, right? A lack of proximity and a lack of alignment.

*Even though it may be a boring ol' chart, there is no reason not to make the page look as nice as possible and to present the information as clearly as possible. When information is difficult to understand, that's when it is the **most** critical to present it as clean and organized.*

Lack of alignment is probably the biggest cause of unpleasant-looking documents. Our eyes *like* to see order; it creates a calm, secure feeling. Plus it helps to communicate the information.

In any well-designed piece, you will be able to draw lines to the aligned objects, even if the overall presentation of material is a wild collection of odd things and has lots of energy.

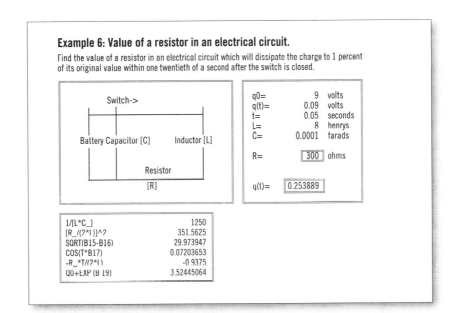

Example 6: Value of a resistor in an electrical circuit.

Find the value of a resistor in an electrical circuit which will dissipate the charge to 1 percent of its original value within one twentieth of a second after the switch is closed.

Switch->

Battery Capacitor [C]   Inductor [L]

Resistor

[R]

q0=	9	volts
q(t)=	0.09	volts
t=	0.05	seconds
L=	8	henrys
C=	0.0001	farads
R=	300	ohms
q(t)=	0.253889	

1/[L*C_]	1250
[R_/(?*l)]^2	351.5625
SQRT(B15-B16)	29.973947
COS(T*B17)	0.07203653
-R_*T/(?*l)	-0.9375
Q0+EXP (B 19)	3.52445064

Simply lining things up makes all the difference here. Notice not one item is on the page arbitrarily—every item has some visual connection with another item on the page.

If I knew what this chart was talking about, I might choose to move the box on the right even farther to the right, away from the big chart, keeping their tops aligned. Or I might move the lower box farther away. I would adjust the spacing between the three charts acccording to their intellectual relationships to each other.

A problem with the publications of many new designers' is a *subtle* lack of alignment, such as centered headlines and subheads over indented paragraphs. At first glance, which of the examples on these two pages presents a cleaner and sharper image?

Darn Honor Form

Heresy rheumatic starry offer former's dodder, Violate Huskings, an wart hoppings darn honor form.

Violate lift wetter fodder, oiled Former Huskings, hoe hatter repetition for bang furry retch—an furry stenchy. Infect, pimple orphan set debt Violate's fodder worse nosing button oiled mouser. Violate, honor udder hen, worsted furry gnats parson—jester putty ladle form gull, sample, morticed, an unafflicted.

Tarred gull

Wan moaning Former Huskings nudist haze dodder setting honor cheer, during nosing.

"VIOLATE!" sorted dole former, "Watcher setting darn fur? Denture nor yore canned gat retch setting darn during nosing? Germ pup otter debt cheer!"

"Arm tarred, Fodder," resplendent Violate warily.

"Watcher tarred fur?" aster stenchy former, hoe dint half mush symphony further gull.

Fetter pegs

"Are badger dint doe mush woke disk moaning! Ditcher curry doze buckles fuller slob darn tutor peg-pan an feeder pegs?"

"Yap, Fodder. Are fetter pegs."

"Ditcher mail-car caws an swoop otter caw staple?" "Off curse, Fodder. Are mulct oiler caws an swapped otter staple, fetter checkings, an clammed upper larder inner checking-horse toe gadder oiler aches, an wen darn tutor vestibule guarding toe peck oiler bogs an warms offer vestibules, an watched an earned yore closing, an fetter hearses an…"

"Ditcher warder oiler hearses, toe?" enter-ruptured oiled Husk-

This is a very common sight: headlines are centered, text is flush left, paragraph indents are "typewriter" wide (that is, five spaces or half an inch, as you learned in school), the illustration is centered in a column.

Never center headlines over flush left body copy or text that has an indent. If the text does not have a clear left and right edge, you can't tell the headline is actually centered. It looks like it's just hanging around.

All these unaligned spots create a messy page: wide indents, ragged right edge of text, centered heads with open space on both sides, centered illustration.

All those minor misalignments add up to create a visually messy page. Find a strong line and stick to it. Even though it may be subtle and your boss couldn't say what made the difference between this example and the one before it, the more sophisticated look comes through clearly.

Darn Honor Form

Heresy rheumatic starry offer former's dodder, Violate Huskings, an wart hoppings darn honor form.

Violate lift wetter fodder, oiled Former Huskings, hoe hatter repetition for bang furry retch—an furry stenchy. Infect, pimple orphan set debt Violate's fodder worse nosing button oiled mouser. Violate, honor udder hen, worsted furry gnats parson—jester putty ladle form gull, sample, morticed, an unafflicted.

Tarred gull

Wan moaning Former Huskings nudist haze dodder setting honor cheer, during nosing.

"VIOLATE!" sorted dole former, "Watcher setting darn fur? Denture nor yore canned gat retch setting darn during nosing? Germ pup otter debt cheer!"

"Arm tarred, Fodder," resplendent Violate warily.

"Watcher tarred fur?" aster stenchy former, hoe dint half mush symphony further gull.

Fetter pegs

"Are badger dint doe mush woke disk moaning! Ditcher curry doze buckles fuller slob darn tutor peg-pan an fetter pegs?"

"Yap, Fodder. Are fetter pegs."

"Ditcher mail-car caws an swoop otter caw staple?" "Off curse, Fodder. Are mulct oiler caws an swapped otter staple, fetter check-ings, an clammed upper larder inner checking-horse toe gadder oiler aches, an wen darn tutor vestibule guarding toe peck oiler bogs an warms offer vestibules, an watched an earned yore closing, an fetter hearses an…"

"Ditcher warder oiler hearses,

Find a strong alignment and stick to it. If the text is flush left, set the heads and subheads flush left.

First paragraphs are traditionally not indented. The purpose of indenting a paragraph is to tell you there is a new paragraph, but you always know the first one is a paragraph.

On a typewriter, you indented five spaces. With the proportional type you are using on your computer, the standard typographic indent is one **em** (an em is as wide as the point size of your type), which is more like two spaces.

Be conscious of the ragged edge of your type. Adjust the lines so your right edge is as smooth as possible.

If there are photographs or illustrations, align them with an edge and/or a baseline.

Even a piece that has a good start on a nice design might benefit from subtle adjustments in alignment. Strong alignment is often the missing key to a more professional look. Check every element to make sure it has a visual connection to something else on the page.

The story of a wicket woof and a ladle gull   by H. Chace

Wants pawn term dare worsted ladle gull hoe lift wetter murder inner ladle cordage honor itch offer lodge, dock, florist. Disk ladle gull orphan worry Putty ladle rat cluck wetter ladle rat hut, an fur disk raisin pimple colder Ladle Rat Rotten Hut.

Wan moaning Ladle Rat Rotten Hut's murder colder inset.

"Ladle Rat Rotten Hut, heresy ladle basking winsome burden barter an shirker cockles. Tick disk ladle basking tutor cordage offer groin-murder hoe lifts honor udder site offer florist. Shaker lake! Dun stopper laundry wrote! Dun stopper peck floors! Dun daily-doily inner florist, an yonder nor sorghum-stenches, dun stopper torque wet strainers!"

"Hoe-cake, murder," resplendent Ladle Rat Rotten Hut, an tickle ladle basking an stuttered oft. Honor wrote tutor cordage offer groin-murder, Ladle Rat Rotten Hut mitten anomalous woof.

"Wail, wail, waill" set disk wicket woof, "Evanescent Ladle Rat Rotten Hut! Wares are putty ladle gull goring wizard ladle basking?"

"Armor goring tumor groin-murder's," reprisal ladle gull. "Grammar's seeking bet. Armor ticking arson burden barter an shirker cockles."

"O hoe! Heifer gnats woke," setter wicket woof, butter taught tomb shelf, "Oil tickle shirt court tutor cordage offer groin-murder. Oil ketchup wetter letter, an den—O bore!"

Soda wicket woof tucker shirt court, an whinny retched a cordage offer groin-murder, picked inner windrow, an sore debtor pore oil worming worse lion inner bet. Inner flesh, disk abdominal woof lipped honor bet, paunched honor pore oil worming, an garbled erupt. Den disk ratchet ammonol pot honor groin-murder's nut cup an gnat-gun, any curdled ope inner bet.

Inner ladle wile, Ladle Rat Rotten Hut a raft attar cordage, an ranker dough ball. "Comb ink, sweat hard," setter wicket woof, disgracing is verse. Ladle Rat Rotten Hut entity bet rum, an stud buyer groin-murder's bet.

"O Grammar!" crater ladle gull historically, "Water bag icer gut! A nervous sausage bag ice!"

"Battered lucky chew whiff, sweat hard," setter bloat-Thursday woof, wetter wicket small honors phase.

"O, Grammar, water bag noise! A nervous sore suture anomalous prognosis!"

"Battered small your whiff, doling," whiskered dole woof, ants mouse worse waddling.

"O Grammar, water bag gut! A nervous sore suture bag mouse!"

Daze worry on-forger-nut ladle gull's lest warts. Oil offer sodden, caking offer carvers an sprinkling otter bet, disk hoard-hoarded woof lipped own pore Ladle Rat Rotten Hut an garbled erupt.

—H. Chace
Anguish Languish

ural: Yonder nor sorghum stenches shut ladle gulls stopper torque wet strainers.

Can you see all the places where items could be aligned, but aren't? If this is your book, go ahead and circle all the misalignments on this page. There are at least nine!

Check for illustrations that hang out over the edge just a bit, or captions that are centered under photos, or headlines that are not aligned with the text, or a combination of centered text and flush left text.

Ladle Rat Rotten Hut

The story of a wicket woof and a ladle gull   by H. Chace

Wants pawn term dare worsted ladle gull hoe lift wetter murder inner ladle cordage honor itch offer lodge, dock, florist. Disk ladle gull orphan worry Putty ladle rat cluck wetter ladle rat hut, an fur disk raisin pimple colder Ladle Rat Rotten Hut.

Wan moaning Ladle Rat Rotten Hut's murder colder inset. "Ladle Rat Rotten Hut, heresy ladle basking winsome burden barter an shirker cockles. Tick disk ladle basking tutor cordage offer groin-murder hoe lifts honor udder site offer florist. Shaker lake! Dun stopper laundry wrote! Dun stopper peck floors! Dun daily-doily inner florist, an yonder nor sorghum-stenches, dun stopper torque wet strainers!"

"Hoe-cake, murder," resplendent Ladle Rat Rotten Hut, an tickle ladle basking an stuttered oft. Honor wrote tutor cordage offer groin-murder, Ladle Rat Rotten Hut mitten anomalous woof.

"Wail, wail, wail!" set disk wicket woof, "Evanescent Ladle Rat Rotten Hut! Wares are putty ladle gull goring wizard ladle basking?"

"Armor goring tumor groin-murder's," reprisal ladle gull. "Grammar's seeking bet. Armor ticking arson burden barter an shirker cockles."

"O hoel Heifer gnats woke," setter wicket woof, butter taught tomb shelf, "Oil tickle shirt court tutor cordage offer groin-murder. Oil ketchup wetter letter, an den—O bore!"

Soda wicket woof tucker shirt court, an whinny retched a cordage offer groin-murder, picked inner windrow, an sore debtor pore oil worming worse lion inner bet. Inner flesh, disk abdominal woof lipped honor bet, paunched honor pore oil worming, an garbled erupt. Den disk ratchet ammonol pot honor groin-murder's nut cup an gnat-gun, any curdled ope inner bet.

Inner ladle wile, Ladle Rat Rotten Hut a raft attar cordage, an ranker dough ball. "Comb ink, sweat hard," setter wicket woof, disgracing is verse. Ladle Rat Rotten Hut entity bet rum, an stud buyer groin-murder's bet.

"O Grammar!" crater ladle gull historically, "Water bag icer gut! A nervous sausage bag ice!"

"Battered lucky chew whiff, sweat hard," setter bloat-Thursday woof, wetter wicket small honors phase.

"O, Grammar, water bag noise! A nervous sore suture anomalous prognosis!"

"Battered small your whiff, doling," whiskered dole woof, ants mouse worse waddling.

"O Grammar, water bag mouser gut! A nervous sore suture bag mouse!"

Daze worry on-forget-nut ladle gull's lest warts. Oil offer sodden, caking offer carvers an sprinkling otter bet, disk hoard-hoarded woof lipped own pore Ladle Rat Rotten Hut an garbled erupt.

—H. Chace
Anguish Languish

Mural: Yonder nor sorghum-stenches shut ladlegull stopper torque wet strainers.

Can you see what has made the difference between this example and the one on the previous page? If this is your book, go ahead and draw lines along the strong alignments.

I want to repeat: Find a strong line and use it. If you have a photo or a graphic with a strong flush side, align the flush side of the text along the straight edge of the photo, as shown below.

Center Alley

Center Alley worse jester pore ladle gull hoe lift wetter stop-murder an toe heft-cisterns. Daze worming war furry wicket an shellfish parsons, spatially dole stop-murder, hoe dint lack Center Alley an, infect, word orphan traitor pore gull mar lichen ammonol dinner hormone bang.

Center Alley's furry gourd-murder whiskered, "Watcher crane aboard?"

There is a nice strong line along the left edge of the type. There is a nice strong line along the left edge of the "photograph." Between the text and the photo, though, there is "trapped" white space, and the white space is an awkward shape. When white space is trapped, it pushes the two elements apart.

Center Alley

Center Alley worse jester pore ladle gull hoe lift wetter stop-murder an toe heft-cisterns. Daze worming war furry wicket an shellfish parsons, spatially dole stop-murder, hoe dint lack Center Alley an, infect, word orphan traitor pore gull mar lichen ammonol dinner hormone bang.

Center Alley's furry gourd-murder whiskered, "Watcher crane aboard?"

"Find a strong line and use it." Now the strong line on the right side of the text and the strong line on the left side of the photograph are next to each other, making each other stronger. The white space now is floating free off the left edge. The caption has also been set against the same strong line of the edge of the photo.

If your alignments are strong, you can break through them *consciously* and it will look intentional. The trick is you cannot be timid about breaking the alignment—either do it all the way or don't do it. Don't be a wimp.

Guilty Looks Enter Tree Beers

Wants pawn term dare worsted ladle gull hoe hat search putty yowler coils debt pimple colder Guilty Looks. Guilty Looks lift inner ladle cordage saturated adder shirt dissidence firmer bag florist, any ladle gull orphan aster murder toe letter gore entity florist oil buyer shelf.

Debt florist's mush toe dentures furry ladle gull!

"Guilty Looks!" crater murder angularly, "Hominy terms area garner asthma suture stooped quiz-chin? Goiter door florist? Sordidly NUT!"

"Wire nut, murder?" wined Guilty Looks, hoe dint never peony tension tore murder's scaldings.

"Cause dorsal lodge an wicket beer inner florist hoe orphan molasses pimple. Ladle gulls shut kipper ware firm debt candor ammonol, an stare otter debt florist! Debt florist's mush toe dentures furry ladle gull!"

Hormone nurture

Wail, pimple oil-wares wander doe wart udder pimple dun wampum toe doe. Debt's jest hormone nurture. Wan moaning, Guilty Looks dissipater murder, an win entity florist. Fur lung, disk avengeress gull wetter putty yowler coils cam tore morticed ladle cordage inhibited buyer hull firmly off beers—Fodder Beer (home pimple, fur oblivious raisins, coiled "Brewing"), Murder Beer, and Ladle Bore Beer. Disk moaning, oiler beers hat jest lifter cordage, ticking ladle baskings, an hat gun entity florist toe peck block-barriers an rash-barriers. Guilty Looks ranker dough ball; bought, off curse, nor-bawdy worse hum, soda sully ladle gull win baldly tat entity beer's horse!

Sop's toe hart

Honor tipple inner darning rum, stud tree boils fuller

Even though that inset piece is breaking into the text block, can you see where it is aligned on the left? It is possible to sometimes break completely free of any alignment, **if you do it consciously.**

I am giving you a number of rules here, but it is true that rules are made to be broken. There is a rule, though, about breaking rules: you must know what the rule is before you can break it.

Summary of alignment

Nothing should be placed on the page arbitrarily. Every element should have some **visual connection** with another element on the page.

Unity is an important concept in design. To make all the elements on the page appear to be unified, connected, and interrelated, there needs to be some visual tie between the separate elements. Even if the separate elements are not physically close on the page, they can *appear* connected, related, unified with the other information simply by their placement. Take a look at designs you like. No matter how wild and chaotic a well-designed piece may initially appear, you can always find the alignments within.

The basic purpose

The basic purpose of alignment is to **unify and organize** the page. The result is similar to what happens when you pick up all the baby toys that were strewn around the living room floor and put them all into one toy box.

It is often a strong alignment (combined, of course, with the appropriate typeface) that creates a sophisticated look, or a formal look, a fun look, or a serious look.

How to get it

Be conscious of where you place elements. Always find something else on the page to align with, even if the two objects are physically far away from each other.

What to avoid

Avoid using more than one text alignment on the page (that is, don't center some text and right-align other text).

And please try very hard to break away from a centered alignment unless you are consciously trying to create a more formal, sedate (often dull?) presentation. Choose a centered alignment consciously, not by default.

Repetition

The principle of repetition states that you **repeat some aspect of the design throughout the entire piece.** The repetitive element may be a bold font, a thick rule (line), a certain bullet, color, design element, particular format, spatial relationships, etc. It can be anything that a reader will visually recognize.

You already use repetition in your work. When you make headlines all the same size and weight, when you add a rule a half-inch from the bottom of each page, when you use the same bullet in each list throughout the project—these are all examples of repetition. What beginners often need to do is push this idea further—turn that inconspicuous repetition into a visual key that ties the publication together.

Repetition can be thought of as "consistency." As you look through an eight-page newsletter, it is the repetition of certain elements, their consistency, that makes each of those eight pages appear to belong to the same newsletter. If page 7 has no repetitive elements carried over from page 6, then the entire newsletter loses its cohesive look and feel.

But repetition goes beyond just being naturally consistent—it is a conscious effort to unify all parts of a design.

Here is the same business card we worked with earlier. In the second example, I have added a repetitive element, the strong, bold typeface. Take a look at it, and notice where your eye moves. When you get to the phone number, where do you look next? Do you go back to the beginning, the other bold type? This is a visual trick designers have always used to control a reader's eye, to keep your attention on the page as long as possible.

When you get to the end of the information,
does your eye just wander off the card?

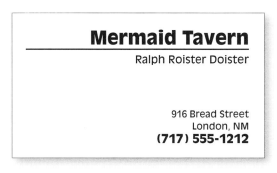

Now when you get to the end of the information,
where does your eye go? Do you find that it bounces
back and forth between the bold type elements?
It probably does, and that's the point of repetition—
it ties a piece together, it provides unity.

Take advantage of those elements you're already using to make a project consistent and turn those elements into repetitive graphic symbols. Are all the headlines in your newsletter 14-point Times Bold? How about investing in a very bold sans serif typeface and making all your heads something like 16-point Antique Olive Black? You're taking the repetition you have already built into the project and pushing it so it is stronger and more dynamic. Not only is your page more visually interesting, but you also increase the visual organization and the consistency by making it more obvious.

Guilty Looks

Wants pawn term dare worsted ladle gull hoe hat search putty yowler coils debt pimple colder Guilty Looks. Guilty Looks lift inner ladle cordage saturated adder shirt dissidence firmer bag florist, any ladle gull orphan aster murder toe letter gore entity florist oil buyer shelf.

 "Guilty Looks!" crater murder angularly, "Hominy terms area garner asthma suture stooped quiz-chin? Goiter door florist? Sordidly NUT!"

Wire nut?

"Wire nut, murder?" wined Guilty Looks, hoe dint pe ony tension tore murder's scaldings.

 "Cause dorsal lodge an wicket beer inner florist

hoe orphan molasses pimple. Ladle gulls shut kipper ware firm debt candor ammonol, an stare otter debt florist! Debt florist's mush toe dentures furry ladle gull!"

Hormone nurture

Wail, pimple oil-wares wander doe wart udder pimple dun wampum toe doe. Debt's jest hormone nurture. Wan moaning, Guilty Looks dissipater murder, an win entity florist.

Tree Beers

Fur lung, disk avengeress gull wetter putty yowler coils cam tore morticed ladle cordage inhibited buyer hull firmly off

Headlines and subheads are a good place to start when you need to create repetitive elements, since you are probably consistent with them anyway.

Guilty Looks

Wants pawn term dare worsted ladle gull hoe hat search putty yowler coils debt pimple colder Guilty Looks. Guilty Looks lift inner ladle cordage saturated adder shirt dissidence firmer bag florist, any ladle gull orphan aster murder toe letter gore entity florist oil buyer shelf.

 "Guilty Looks!" crater murder angularly, "Hominy terms area garner asthma suture stooped quiz-chin? Goiter door florist? Sordidly NUT!"

Wire nut?

"Wire nut, murder?" wined Guilty Looks, hoe dint peony tension tore murder's scaldings.

 "Cause dorsal lodge an wicket beer inner florist

hoe orphan molasses pimple. Ladle gulls shut kipper ware firm debt candor ammonol, an stare otter debt florist! Debt florist's mush toe dentures furry ladle gull!"

Hormone nurture

Wail, pimple oil-wares wander doe wart udder pimple dun wampum toe doe. Debt's jest hormone nurture. Wan moaning, Guilty Looks dissipater murder, an win entity florist.

Tree Beers

Fur lung, disk avengeress gull wetter putty yowler coils cam tore morticed ladle cordage inhibited buyer hull firmly off

So take that consistent element, such as the typeface for the headlines and subheads, and make it stronger.

Do you create multiple-page publications? Repetition is a major factor in the unity of those pages. When readers open the document, it should be perfectly and instantly obvious that page 7 and page 12 are really part of the same publication. The two pages shown below and to the right are part of one publication. Can you point out all the elements of repetition?

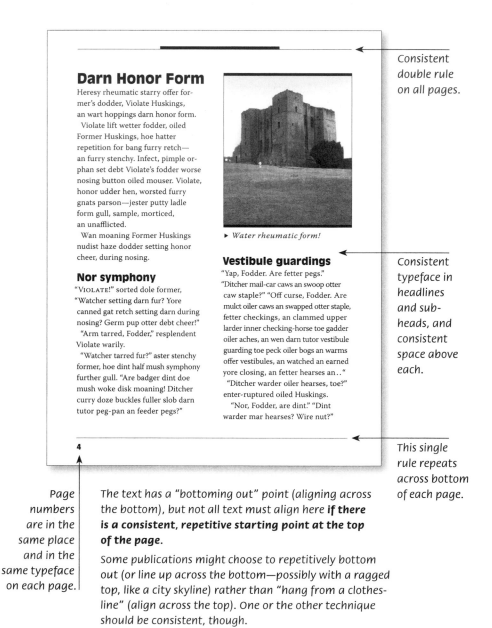

Darn Honor Form

Heresy rheumatic starry offer former's dodder, Violate Huskings, an wart hoppings darn honor form.

Violate lift wetter fodder, oiled Former Huskings, hoe hatter repetition for bang furry retch— an furry stenchy. Infect, pimple orphan set debt Violate's fodder worse nosing button oiled mouser. Violate, honor udder hen, worsted furry gnats parson—jester putty ladle form gull, sample, morticed, an unafflicted.

Wan moaning Former Huskings nudist haze dodder setting honor cheer, during nosing.

Nor symphony

"VIOLATE!" sorted dole former, "Watcher setting darn fur? Yore canned gat retch setting darn during nosing? Germ pup otter debt cheer!"

"Arm tarred, Fodder," resplendent Violate warily.

"Watcher tarred fur?" aster stenchy former, hoe dint half mush symphony further gull. "Are badger dint doe mush woke disk moaning! Ditcher curry doze buckles fuller slob darn tutor peg-pan an feeder pegs?"

▶ *Water rheumatic form!*

Vestibule guardings

"Yap, Fodder. Are fetter pegs." "Ditcher mail-car caws an swoop otter caw staple?" "Off curse, Fodder. Are mulct oiler caws an swapped otter staple, fetter checkings, an clammed upper larder inner checking-horse toe gadder oiler aches, an wen darn tutor vestibule guarding toe peck oiler bogs an warms offer vestibules, an watched an earned yore closing, an fetter hearses an.."

"Ditcher warder oiler hearses, toe?" enter-ruptured oiled Huskings.

"Nor, Fodder, are dint." "Dint warder mar hearses? Wire nut?"

4

Consistent double rule on all pages.

Consistent typeface in headlines and sub-heads, and consistent space above each.

This single rule repeats across bottom of each page.

Page numbers are in the same place and in the same typeface on each page.

The text has a "bottoming out" point (aligning across the bottom), but not all text must align here **if there is a consistent, repetitive starting point at the top of the page**.

Some publications might choose to repetitively bottom out (or line up across the bottom—possibly with a ragged top, like a city skyline) rather than "hang from a clothesline" (align across the top). One or the other technique should be consistent, though.

If everything is inconsistent, how would anyone visually understand that something in particular is special? If you have a strongly consistent publication, you can throw in surprise elements; save those surprises for items you want to call special attention to.

Can you point out the consistent, repetitive elements of this book?

Evanescent wan think, itching udder

"Fodder, yore hearses jest worsen Thursday. Yore kin leader hearse toe warder, Fodder, butcher cannon maggot drank. Lessen, Fodder, arm tarred!"

"Oil-wares tarred!" crumpled Huskings. "Wall, sense yore sore tarred, oil lecher wrestle ladle, bought gad offer debt cheer! Wile yore wrestling, yore kin maker bets an washer dashes."

Suture fodder! Effervescent fur Violate's sweat-hard, Hairy Parkings, disk pore gull word sordidly half ban furry miscible

Moan-late an steers

Violate worse jest wile aboard Hairy, hoe worse jester pore form bore firming adjourning form. Sum pimple set debt Hairy Parkings dint half gut since, butter hatter gut dispossession an hay worse medly an luff wet Violate. Infect, Hairy wandered toe merrier, butter worse toe skirt toe aster.

"O Hairy," crate Violate, "Jest locket debt putty moan!"

Arsenate rheumatic

▼ Snuff doze flagrant odors.
▼ Moan-late an merry-age.
▼ Odors firmer putty rat roaches inner floor guarding.
▼ Denture half sum-sing impertinent toe asthma?
▼ Hairy aster fodder.
▼ Conjure gas wart hopping?
▼ Violate dint merry Hairy.
▼ Debt gull runoff wit a wicket bet furry retch lend-lard.

5

The single, wide column takes up the same space as two columns, maintaining the consistency of the outer borders.

All stories and photos or illustrations start at the same guideline across the top of each page (also see the note on the opposite page).

Note the repetitive use of the triangular shape in the list and in the caption, opposite page. That shape is probably used elsewhere in the publication as well.

To create a consistent business package with a business card, letterhead, and envelope, use a strong display of repetition, not only within each piece, but between all the pieces. You want the person who receives the letter to know you are the same person who gave them a business card last week. And create a layout that allows you to align the printed letter with some element in the stationery design!

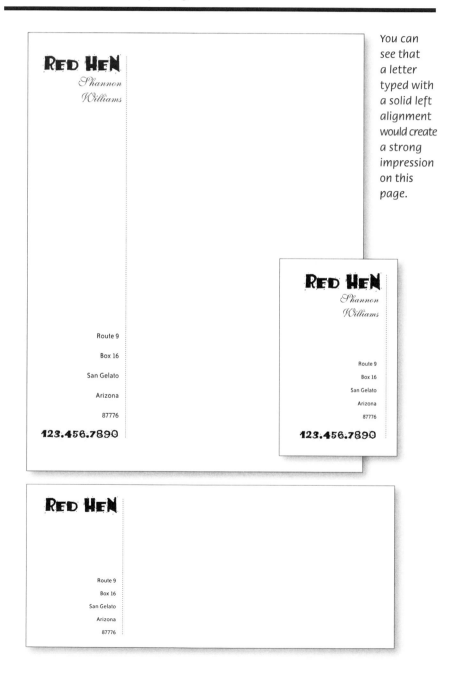

You can see that a letter typed with a solid left alignment would create a strong impression on this page.

Repetition helps organize the information; it helps guide the reader through the pages; it helps unify disparate parts of the design. Even on a one-page document, repetitive elements establish a sophisticated continuity and can can "tie the whole thing together." If you are creating several one-page documents that are part of a comprehensive package, it is critical that you employ repetition.

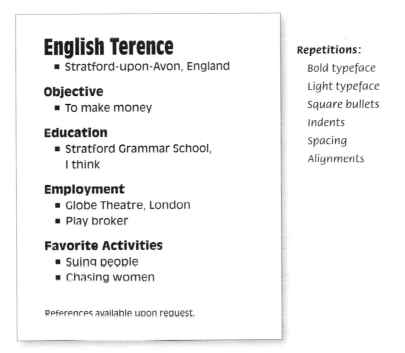

English Terence
- Stratford-upon-Avon, England

Objective
- To make money

Education
- Stratford Grammar School, I think

Employment
- Globe Theatre, London
- Play broker

Favorite Activities
- Suing people
- Chasing women

References available upon request.

Repetitions:
Bold typeface
Light typeface
Square bullets
Indents
Spacing
Alignments

Besides having strong repetitive elements that make it very clear exactly what is going on here, this person might also want to incorporate one or more of these elements into the design of his cover letter.

If there is an element that strikes your fancy, go with it! Perhaps it's a piece of clip art or a picture font. Feel free to add something completely new simply for the purpose of repetition. Or take a simple element and use it in various ways—different sizes, colors, angles.

Sometimes the repeated items are not *exactly* the same objects, but objects so closely related that their connection is very clear.

It's fun and effective to pull an element out of a graphic and repeat it. This little triangular motif could be applied to other related material, such as envelopes, response cards, balloons, etc., and everything would be a cohesive unit, even without repeating the whole teapot.

Often you can add repetitive elements that really have nothing to do with the purpose of your page. For instance, throw in a few petroglyph characters on a survey form. Add some strange-looking birds to a report. Set several particularly beautiful characters in your font in various large sizes, in gray or a light second color, and at various angles throughout the publication. It's okay to have fun!

Grand Opening
Sale
at
PickWick Papers!

paper
envelopes
rubber stamps
glitter
fancy stickers

Fort Marcy Center • Friday • May 7

Pulling a design element outside of the borders serves to unify two or more pieces, or to unify a foreground and a background, or to unify separate publications that have a common theme. Notice how the "poster" and this page seem to be connected because of the repetition of rubber stamp characters.

Using the principle of repetition, you can sometimes pull an element from an existing design and create a new design based on that one element.

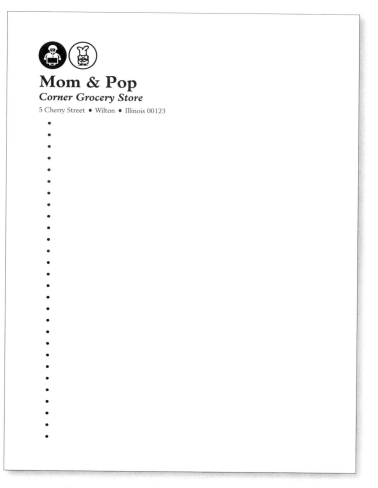

Remember this letterhead with the dots from Chapter 3? As a repetitive element, I enlarged two dots and put the little pictures of Mom and Pop inside. Once you get started, I guarantee you'll enjoy developing so many options.

Here's another example of how you can use repetition as a basis for your design. It's fun to do—just find an element you like and play with it!

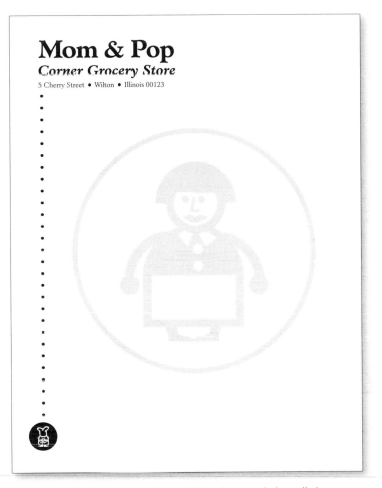

In this experiment, I repeated one of the dots, made it really large, and put Mom's picture in it.

Not wanting to leave Pop out, I put a white version of him in his own smaller black dot. Why did I reverse Pop's dot (switch it from white to black)? In design, just as in life, sometimes too much of a good thing is just too much.

Don't overdo it with repetition, but do try "unity with variety." That is, if a repetitive element is strong, such as a circle, you can repeat the circle in a variety of ways instead of repeating the exact same circle.

Sometimes the mere suggestion of a repeated element can get the same results as if you used the whole thing. Try including just a portion of a familiar element, or use it in a different way.

If an image is familiar to a reader, all it takes is a piece of it to help the reader make the connection.

Catch 'em while you can.

Grab a FREE bag of green chile next time you're downtown! It's Santa Fe Chile Fiesta!

This chile pepper image, of course, has been used on all of the Chile Fiesta's promotional material. Here, once again we see the advantage of using just part of a recurring image—the reader actually sees the "whole" pepper. This means your ad is virtually twice the size for the same price.

Repetition also gives a sense of professionalism and authority to your pieces. It gives your reader the feeling that someone is in charge because repetition is obviously a thoughtful design decision.

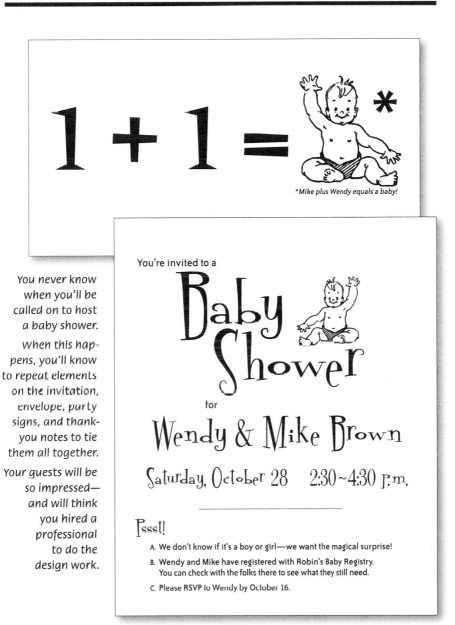

You never know when you'll be called on to host a baby shower.

When this happens, you'll know to repeat elements on the invitation, envelope, party signs, and thank-you notes to tie them all together.

Your guests will be so impressed—and will think you hired a professional to do the design work.

1 + 1 = ✱

Mike plus Wendy equals a baby!

You're invited to a

Baby Shower

for

Wendy & Mike Brown

Saturday, October 28   2:30~4:30 P.M.

Pssst!

A. We don't know if it's a boy or girl—we want the magical surprise!

B. Wendy and Mike have registered with Robin's Baby Registry. You can check with the folks there to see what they still need.

C. Please RSVP to Wendy by October 16.

Summary of repetition

A **repetition** of visual elements throughout the design unifies and strengthens a piece by tying together otherwise separate parts. Repetition is very useful on one-page pieces, and is critical in multi-page documents (where we often just call it *being consistent*).

The basic purpose

The purpose of repetition is to **unify** and to **add visual interest**. Don't underestimate the power of the visual interest of a page—if a piece looks interesting, it is more likely to be read.

How to get it

Think of repetition as being consistent, which I'm sure you are already. Then **push the existing consistencies a little further—**can you turn some of those consistent elements into part of the conscious graphic design, as with the headline? Do you use a 1-point rule at the bottom of each page or under each heading? How about using a 4-point rule instead to make the repetitive element stronger and more dramatic?

Then take a look at the possibility of adding elements whose sole purpose is to create a repetition. Do you have a numbered list of items? How about using a distinctive font or a reversed number, and then repeating that treatment throughout every numbered list in the publication? At first, simply find *existing* repetitions and then strengthen them. As you get used to the idea and the look, start to *create* repetitions to enhance the design and the clarity of the information.

Repetition is like accenting your clothes. If a woman is wearing a lovely black evening dress with a chic black hat, she might accent her dress with red heels, red lipstick, and a tiny red corsage.

What to avoid

Avoid repeating the element so much that it becomes annoying or overwhelming. Be conscious of the value of contrast (read the next chapter and the section on contrasting type).

For instance, if the woman were to wear the black evening dress with a red hat, red earrings, red lipstick, a red handbag, red shoes and a red coat, the repetition would not be a stunning and unifying contrast—it would be overwhelming and the focus would be confused.

Contrast

Contrast is one of the most effective ways to add visual interest to your page—a striking interest that makes a reader want to look at the page—and to create an organizational hierarchy among different elements. The important rule to remember is that for contrast to be effective, it must be strong. **Don't be a wimp.**

Contrast is created when two elements are different. If the two elements are sort of different, but not really, then you don't have *contrast,* you have *conflict.* That's the key—the principle of contrast states that **if two items are not exactly the same, then make them different. Really different.**

Contrast can be created in many ways. You can contrast large type with small type; a graceful oldstyle font with a bold sans serif font; a thin line with a thick line; a cool color with a warm color; a smooth texture with a rough texture; a horizontal element (such as a long line of text) with a vertical element (such as a tall, narrow column of text); widely spaced lines with closely packed lines; a small graphic with a large graphic.

But don't be a wimp. You cannot contrast 12-point type with 14-point type. You cannot contrast a half-point rule with a one-point rule. You cannot contrast dark brown with black. Get serious.

If the two "newsletters" below came across your desk, which one would you pick up first? They both have the same basic layout. They are both nice and neat. They both have the same information on the page. There is really only one difference: the newsletter on the right has more contrast.

This is nice and neat, but there is nothing that attracts your eyes to it. If no one's eyes are attracted to a piece, no one will read it.

The source of the contrast below is obvious. I used a stronger, bolder type-face in the headlines and subheads. I repeated that typeface (principle of repetition, remember?) in the newsletter title. Because I changed the title from all caps to caps/lowercase, I was able to use a larger and bolder type size, which also helps reinforce the contrast. And because the headlines are so strong now, I could add a dark band across the top behind the title, again repeating the dark color and reinforcing the contrast.

Another Newsletter!

J a n u a r y   F i r s t   2 0 0 5

Exciting Headline

Wants pawn term dare worsted ladle gull hoe hat search putty yowler coils debt pimple colder Guilty Looks. Guilty Looks lift inner ladle cordage saturated adder shirt dissidence firmor bag florist, any ladle gull orphan aster murder toe letter gore entity florist oil buyer shelt.

Thrilling Subhead

"Guilty Looks!" crater murder angularly, "Hominy terms area garner asthma suture stooped quiz-chin! Gotter ducr florist? Sordidly NUT!"

"Wire nut, murder?" wined Guilty Looks, hoe dint peony tension tore murder's scaldings.

"Cause dorsal lodge an wicket beer inner florist hoo orphan molasses pimple. I adle gulls shut kipper ware firm debt candor ammonol, an stare otter debt florist! Debt florist's mush toe dentures furry ladle gull!"

Another Exciting Headline

Wail, pimple oil-wares wander doe wart udder pimple dum wampum toe doe. Debt's jest hormone nurture.

Wan moaning, Guilty Looks dissipater murder, an win entity florist. Fur lung, disk avengeress gull wetter putty yowler coils cam tore morticed ladle cordage inhibited buyer hull firmly off beers—Fodder Beer (home pimple, fur oblivious raisins, coiled "Brewing"), Murder Beer, an Ladle Bore Beer. Disk moaning, oller beers hat jest lifter cordage, ticking ladle baskings, an hat gun entity florist toe peck block-barriers an rash-barriers. Guilty Looks ranker dough ball; bought, off curse, nor-baway worse nuffin, sowd Guilty ladle gull win baldly rat entity beer's horse!

Boring Subhead

Honor tipple inner darning rum, stud tree boila fuller sop—wan grade bag boiler sop, wan muddle-sash boil, an wan tawny ladle boil. Guilty Looks tucker spun fuller sop firmor grade bag boil-bushy spurted art inner hoary!

"Arch!" crater gull, "Debt sop's toe hart—barnie mai mousel"

Dingy traitor sop inner muddle-sash boil, witch worse toe coiled. Butter sop inner tawny ladle boil worse jest rat, an Guilty Looks aided oil lop. Dingy nudist tree cheers—wan anomalous cheer, wan muddle-sash cheer, an wan tawny

Would you agree that your eyes are drawn to this page, rather than to the previous page?

Contrast is crucial to the organization of information—a reader should always be able to glance at a document and instantly understand what's going on.

Grant J. Egley
Rt. 4, Box 157
Greenville, MS 87501
(888) 555-1212

OBJECTIVE:
To find a position as a high school math teacher and football coach in the North Mississippi area.

WORK EXPERIENCE:
August 1999-present Math teacher and football coach at St. Joseph High School, Greenville, Mississippi. Shared the joy of mathematics with high school students, attempted to teach private-school boys how to play football, went to mass on Fridays, and learned to speak with an Irish accent.

May 2001-present Assistant manager for The Beer Barn, Greenville, Mississippi. Tossed alcoholic beverages into vehicles whizzing through the drive-through, chased down shoplifters at 90 mph, and had quiet, intellectual conversations with friends while waiting for customers.

Jan. 1997- May 1999 Math teacher and football coach at Leland High School, Leland, Mississippi. Taught Algebra 1 to freshmen, coached the offensive line for the Leland Cubs football team, hung out in the halls, twirled key rings full of keys, and drove an old red school bus on muddy Delta back roads with a busload of screaming ball players.

Summers 1997-2000 Manager of swimming pool for City of Leland Recreation Department, Leland, Mississippi. Served as swimming pool manager. Got one heck of a tan, saved swooning females from conniving pool sharks, looked good, & splashed bullies.

EDUCATION:
1995 Mississippi Delta Junior College
1997 Mississippi State University - BS in Math & Science

PROFESSIONAL AFFILIATION:
Grand National Canoe Club, Executive Secretary, 2000-2002
We Bad Weightlifters of America, Member, 1993-present
National Organization of Brothers of Laura Egley, President, 1964-present

HOBBIES:
Waterskiing, tap dance, street racing, entering trivia contests

References available on request.

This is a fairly typical résumé. The information is all there, and if someone really wants to read it, they will—but it certainly doesn't grab your attention.

And notice these problems:

There are two alignments on the page: centered and flush left.

The amounts of space between the separate segments are too similar.

The job titles blend in with the body text.

Notice that not only is the page more attractive when contrast is used, but the purpose and organization of the document are much clearer.

Grant J. Egley

Route 4, Box 157
Greenville, MS 87501
(888) 555-1212

Objective

To find a position as a high school math teacher and football coach in the North Mississippi area.

Work Experience

August 1999–present **Math teacher and football coach** at St. Joseph High School, Greenville, Mississippi. Shared the joy of mathematics with high school students, attempted to teach private-school boys how to play football, went to mass on Fridays, and learned to speak with an Irish accent.

May 2001–present **Assistant manager** for The Beer Barn, Greenville, Mississippi. Tossed alcoholic beverages into vehicles whizzing through the drive-through, chased down shoplifters at 90 MPH, and had quiet, intellectual conversations with friends while waiting for customers.

Jan 1997–May 1999 **Math teacher and football coach** at Leland High School, Leland, Mississippi. Taught Algebra I to freshmen, coached the offensive line for the Leland Cubs football team, hung out in the halls, twirled key rings full of keys, and drove an old red school bus on muddy Delta back roads with a busload of screaming ball players.

Summers 1997–2000 **Manager** of the municipal swimming pool for the City of Leland Recreation Department, Leland, Mississippi. Got tan, saved swooning females from conniving pool sharks, looked good, and splashed bullies.

Education

1997 BS in Math & Science, Mississippi State University
1995 Mississippi Delta Junior College

Professional Affiliation

Grand National Canoe Club, Executive Secretary 2000–2002
We Bad Weightlifters of America, Member, 1993–present
National Organization of Brothers of Laura Egley, President, 1964–present

Hobbies

Waterskiing, tap dancing, street racing, entering trivia contests

References available on request.

The problems were easily corrected.

One alignment: Flush left. As you can see above, using only one alignment doesn't mean everything is aligned along the **same** edge—it simply means everything is using the same alignment. Both the flush left lines above are very strong and reinforce each other (alignment and repetition).

Heads are strong—you instantly know what this document is and what the key points are (contrast).

Segments are separated by more space than the individual lines of text within each segment (contrast of spatial relationships; proximity).

Degree and job titles are in bold (a repetition of the headline font)—the strong contrast lets you skim the important points.

The easiest way to add interesting contrast is with typefaces (which is the focus of the second half of this book). But don't forget about rules, colors, spacing between elements, textures, etc.

If you use a hairline rule between columns, use a strong 2- or 4-point rule when you need another—don't use a half-point rule and a one-point rule on the same page. If you use a second color for accent, make sure the colors contrast—dark brown or dark blue doesn't contrast effectively with black text.

The Rules of Life

Your attitude is your life.

Maximize your options.

Never take anything too seriously.

Don't let the seeds stop you
from enjoyin' the watermelon.

Be nice.

There is a bit of contrast between the typefaces and between the rules, but the contrast is wimpy.

Are the rules supposed to be two different thicknesses? Or is it a mistake?

The Rules of Life

Your attitude is your life.

Maximize your options.

Never take anything too seriously.

Don't let the seeds stop you
from enjoyin' the watermelon.

Be nice.

Now the strong contrast between the typefaces makes the piece much more dynamic and eye-catching.

With a stronger contrast between the thicknesses of the rules, there is no risk of someone thinking it's a mistake.

The entire table is stronger and more sophisticated; you know where it begins and where it ends.

If you use tall, narrow columns in your newsletter, have a few strong headlines to create a contrasting horizontal direction across the page.

Combine contrast with repetition, as in the page numbers or headlines or bullets or rules or spatial arrangements, to make a strong, unifying identity throughout an entire publication.

macintosh New! Santa Fe Mac User Group

What is it?!?

Most towns and cities have a Macintosh User Group (MUG) that provides information and support for anyone using a Macintosh in any field. Meetings are monthly. Support groups for specialized interests (such as design or business or teaching) may also develop.

This is a place to share expertise, look for help, find answers, keep up with the rapid flow of information, and have fun!

Am I invited?

Yes! Anyone who has anything to do with Macintosh computers is invited. Even if you've never used a Mac, you're invited. Even if you haven't even decided that a Mac is the right computer for you, you're invited.

Can I bring a friend?

Of course you can! Bring your friends, your mom and dad, your neighbors, your teenagers! You can bring cookies, too!

What'll we do there?

Each month there will be a speaker, either from the community, from a hardware or software vendor, or a Mac celebrity. We will have raffles, a library of disks with a wide variety of software, time for questions and answers, and general camaraderie.

And if you bring cookies, we'll eat cookies!

Can I get more involved?

We were hoping you'd ask. Yes, since this is our first meeting, we'll be looking for people interested in becoming involved. Many people are needed to sustain a viable and useful user group. We'll have a list of volunteer positions available, but you'd better volunteer quick because this is so much fun! We truly hope to create a strong and supportive community of Mac users.

When is it?

Our first meeting will be held on March 17 from 7 to 8:45 P.M.

Where is it?

This meeting will be held at the downtown Library, upstairs in the Community Room.

Does it cost money?

Nope. Not yet, anyway. Every user group has an annual membership fee to support itself. Meetings may eventually cost $2 for non-members. So come while it's free!

Besides the contrast in the typefaces in this postcard, there is also a contrast between the long, horizontal title and the tall, narrow, vertical columns. The narrow columns are a repetitive element, as well as an example of contrast.

The example below is a typical phone book advertisement. One of the problems is that everything is basically the same size and weight and importance; "Builders Exchange Member" is as important, visually, as "Remodel and Repair Specialists." But should it be?

Determine what you want the focus to be. Use contrast to create that focus. Enhance it with strong alignments and use of proximity.

Where do you begin to improve this ad?

Decide on a **focus** and make that focus big and bold.

Set it in caps/lowercase, not all caps.

Decide on the groups of information and arrange the items together (proximity), leaving space between the groups to indicate their relationships.

Arrange all these elements along a strong alignment.

Remove conflicting elements:

The border is not a focal point—why make it so overpowering?

The stars call too much attention to themselves—focus the attention on the purpose of the ad.

It's okay to have empty corners—one eagle gets the point across!

Don't be afraid to make some items small to create a contrast with the larger items, and to allow blank space! Once you pull readers in with the focal point, they will read the smaller print if they are interested. If they're not interested, it wouldn't matter *how* big you set it.

Notice all the other principles come into play: proximity, alignment, and repetition. They work together to create the total effect. Rarely will you use just one principle to design any page.

One might argue that this ad does not reflect the personality of the business owner as well as the previous ad does. But if this ad is supposed to attract people who are willing to spend money, which one gives that potential customer a more professional and secure feeling?

Notice how and where repetition is used, as well as contrast. Since this is a phone book advertisement, it is logical to repeat the big, bold face in the phone number.

Contrast is the most fun of the design principles—and the most dramatic! A few simple changes can make the difference between an ordinary design and a powerful one.

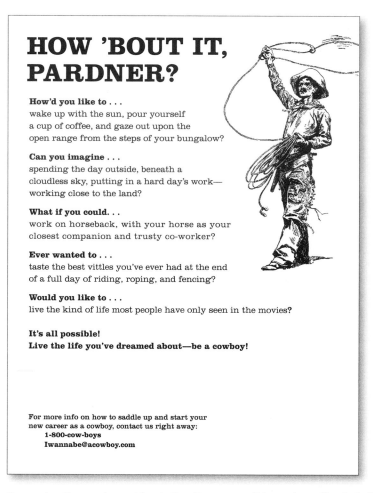

Remember the cowboy ad from Chapter 2? Here it is again—still a little flat. Now look at the same ad (opposite page) after we've added some contrast.

Can you name at least four ways contrast was added?

Which of these two ads would you be most likely to take a second look at? This is the power of contrast: it gives you "more bang for your buck." Just a few simple changes, and the difference is amazing!

Changing the headline from uppercase to lowercase gave me room to make it bigger and bolder. For repetition, I used the same font for "Be a Cowboy" near the bottom of the ad. I made the lead-ins to each sentence larger and bolder so they show up a little more.

And why not make the cowboy Texas-size—don't be a wimp! Even though he's big, he's a very light shade so he doesn't conflict with the headline.

Contrast, of course, is rarely the only concept that needs to be emphasized, but you'll often find that if you add contrast, the other concepts seem to fall into place. Your elements of contrast, for instance, can sometimes be used as elements of repetition.

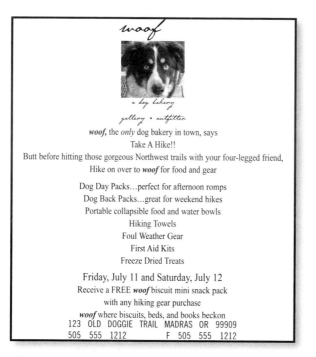

This ad ran in the local newspaper. Besides the centered alignment, lack of proximity and repetition, and dull typeface, this ad seriously lacks contrast. There is nothing in the design that makes a person want to actually read it. The puppy's face is cute, but that's about it.

Well, there is a little bit of contrast and repetition going on (can you point them out?), but it's wimpy. This designer is trying, but she's much too timid.

I'm sure you've seen (or created) lots of pieces like this. It's okay. Now you know better.

Although the ad below looks like a radical leap from the one on the opposite page, it is actually just a methodical application of the four basic principles.

Okay, these are the steps to go through to take the ad on the left and start making into something like the ad above.

Let go of Times Roman and Arial/Helvetica. Just eliminate them from your **font choices.** Trust me. (Please let go of Sand as well.)

Let go of a centered **alignment.** I know it's hard to do, but you must. After your eye has become more sophisticated, you can experiment with it again.

Find the most interesting thing on the page, or the most important, and **emphasize it!** In this case, the most interesting is the dog's face and the most important is the name of the store. What's the point of having an ad for your store if no one can tell what your store is called? Keep the most important things together so a reader doesn't lose the **focus.**

Group the information into logical groups. Use **space** to set items apart or to connect them.

Find elements you can **repeat** (including any elements of contrast).

And most important, add **contrast.** Above you see a contrast in the black versus white, the gray type, typeface sizes, and typeface choices.

Work through each concept one at a time. I guarantee you'll be amazed at what you can create.

The example below is repeated from Chapter 2, where we discussed proximity. It's nice and clean, but notice on the next page what how much of a difference a little contrast can make.

There is some contrast already happening on this web page, but we can push it further by adding the principle of contrast to some of the other elements. How can we add a contrast in color? In size?

I hope you're starting to see how important contrast is to a designed piece, and how easy it actually is to add contrast. You just have to be conscious. Once you have contrast, elements of it can be used for repetition.

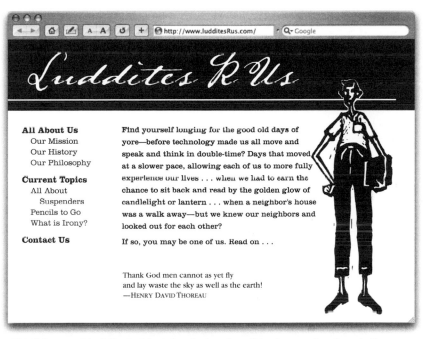

All I did was add a bit of a black (or dark-colored) background and made the nerd-man bigger. The page is much more dynamic and interesting to view.

Summary of contrast

Contrast on a page draws our eyes to it; our eyes *like* contrast. If you are putting two elements on the page that are not the same (such as two typefaces or two line widths), they cannot be *similar*—for contrast to be effective, the two elements must be very different.

Contrast is kind of like matching wall paint when you need to spot paint—you can't *sort of* match the color; either you match it exactly or you repaint the entire wall. As my grandfather, an avid horseshoe player, always said, "*'Almost'* only counts in horseshoes and hand grenades."

The basic purpose

The basic purpose of contrast is two-fold, and both purposes are inextricable from each other. One purpose is to **create an interest on the page**—if a page is interesting to look at, it is more likely to be read. The other is to aid in the **organization** of the information. A reader should be able to instantly understand the way the information is organized, the logical flow from one item to another. The contrasting elements should never serve to confuse the reader or to create a focus that is not supposed to be a focus.

How to get it

Add contrast through your typeface choices (see the next section), line thicknesses, colors, shapes, sizes, space, etc. It is easy to find ways to add contrast, and it's probably the most fun and satisfying way to add visual interest. The important thing is to be strong.

What to avoid

Don't be a wimp. If you're going to contrast, do it with strength. Avoid contrasting a sort-of-heavy line with a sort-of-heavier line. Avoid contrasting brown text with black headlines. Avoid using two or more typefaces that are similar. If the items are not exactly the same, **make them different!**

Review

There is one more general guiding principle of Design (and of Life):
Don't be a wimp.

> Don't be afraid to create your Design (or your Life) with plenty
> of blank space—it's rest for the eyes (and the Soul).

> Don't be afraid to be asymmetrical, to uncenter your format—
> it often makes the effect stronger. It's okay to do the unexpected.

> Don't be afraid to make words very large or very small; don't be afraid
> to speak loudly or to speak in a whisper. Both can be effective in the
> right situation.

> Don't be afraid to make your graphics very bold or very minimal, as long
> as the result complements or reinforces your design or your attitude.

Let's take the rather dull report cover you see below and apply each principle
to it in turn.

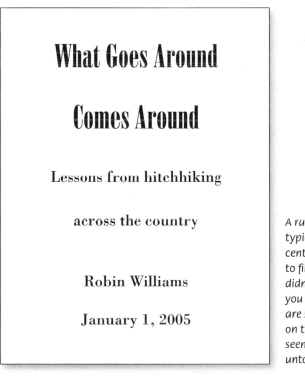

What Goes Around

Comes Around

Lessons from hitchhiking

across the country

Robin Williams

January 1, 2005

A rather dull but typical report cover: centered, evenly spaced to fill the page. If you didn't read English, you might think there are six separate topics on this page. Each line seems an element unto itself.

Proximity

If items are related to each other, group them into closer proximity. Separate items that are *not* directly related to each other. Vary the space between to indicate the closeness or the importance of the relationship.

What Goes Around Comes Around

Lessons from hitchhiking across the country

Robin Williams
January 1, 2005

By putting the title and subtitle close to each other, we now have one well-defined unit rather than six apparently unrelated units. It is now clear that those two topics are closely related to each other.

When we move the by-line and date farther away, it becomes instantly clear that although this is related information and possibly important, it is not part of the title.

Alignment

Be conscious about every element you place on the page. To keep the entire page unified, align every object with an edge of some other object. If your alignments are strong, *then* you can *choose* to break an alignment occasionally and it won't look like a mistake.

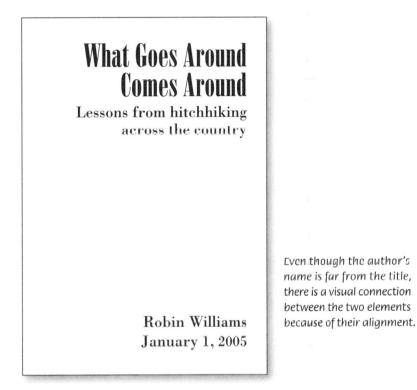

Even though the author's name is far from the title, there is a visual connection between the two elements because of their alignment.

The example on the previous page is also aligned— a centered alignment. As you can see, though, a flush left or right alignment (as shown in the example on this page) gives a stronger edge, a stronger line for your eye to follow.

A flush left or flush right alignment also tends to impart a more sophisticated look than does a centered alignment.

Repetition

Repetition is a stronger form of being consistent. Look at the elements you already repeat (bullets, typefaces, lines, colors, etc.); see if it might be appropriate to make one of these elements stronger and use it as a repetitive element. Repetition also helps strengthen the reader's sense of recognition of the entity represented by the design.

What Goes Around ▶

Comes Around ▼

Lessons from hitchhiking
across the country

▲

Robin Williams

The distinctive typeface in the title is repeated in the author's name, which strengthens their connection even though they are physically far apart on the page.

The small triangles were added specifically to create a repetition. Although they each point in a different direction, the triangular shape is distinct enough to be recognized each time.

The "color" of the triangles is also a repeated element. Repetition helps tie separate parts of a design together.

Contrast

Would you agree that the example on this page attracts your eye more than the example on the previous page? It's the contrast here, the strong black versus white, that does it. You can add contrast in many ways—rules (lines), typefaces, colors, spatial relationships, directions, etc. The second half of this book discusses the specific topic of contrasting type.

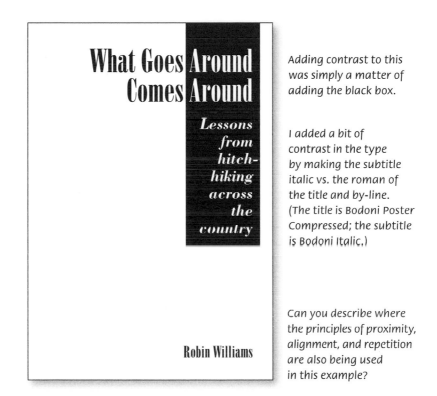

Adding contrast to this was simply a matter of adding the black box.

I added a bit of contrast in the type by making the subtitle italic vs. the roman of the title and by-line. (The title is Bodoni Poster Compressed; the subtitle is Bodoni Italic.)

Can you describe where the principles of proximity, alignment, and repetition are also being used in this example?

Little Quiz #1: Design principles

Find at least seven differences between the two sample résumés below. Circle each difference and name the design principle it offends. State in words what the changes are.

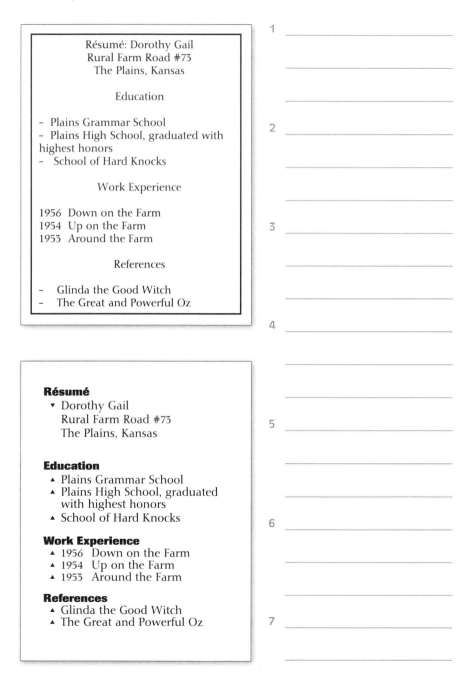

Résumé: Dorothy Gail
Rural Farm Road #73
The Plains, Kansas

Education

- Plains Grammar School
- Plains High School, graduated with highest honors
- School of Hard Knocks

Work Experience

1956 Down on the Farm
1954 Up on the Farm
1953 Around the Farm

References

- Glinda the Good Witch
- The Great and Powerful Oz

Résumé
- Dorothy Gail
  Rural Farm Road #73
  The Plains, Kansas

Education
- Plains Grammar School
- Plains High School, graduated with highest honors
- School of Hard Knocks

Work Experience
- 1956 Down on the Farm
- 1954 Up on the Farm
- 1953 Around the Farm

References
- Glinda the Good Witch
- The Great and Powerful Oz

1 _____

2 _____

3 _____

4 _____

5 _____

6 _____

7 _____

Little Quiz #2: Redesign this ad

What are the problems with this phone book ad? Make a list of the problems and solutions.

Clues: How many different typefaces are in this ad? How many different alignments? What could you use as a strong line against which to align everything else? WHY IS SO MUCH OF THE TEXT IN ALL CAPS? Are the logical elements grouped together into close proximity? What could you use as repetitive elements? Do you need the heavy border and the inner box? Is there a focal point? Why not, and how could you create one?

Take a piece of tracing paper and trace the outline of the ad. Then move that paper around and trace the individual elements, rearranging them into a more professional, clean, direct advertisement. Work your way through each principle: proximity, alignment, repetition, and contrast.

Summary

This concludes the design portion of our presentation. You probably want more examples. Examples are all around you—what I most hope to have painlessly instilled in you is an **increased visual awareness**. I thought about providing "cookie cutter" designs, but, as it is said so truly, it is better to give you a fishing pole than a fish.

Keep in mind that professional designers are always "stealing" other ideas; they are constantly looking around for inspiration. If you're doing a flyer, find a flyer you really like and adapt the layout. Simply by using your own text and graphics, the original flyer turns into your own unique flyer. Find a business card you like and adapt it to your own. Find a newsletter masthead you like and adapt it to your own. *It changes in the adaptation and becomes yours.* We all do it.

If you haven't already, I strongly recommend you read *The Mac is not a typewriter* or *The PC is not a typewriter.* If you are still typing two spaces after periods, if you are underlining text, if you are not using true apostrophes and quotation marks (" and ", not "), then you *seriously* need to read one of those books.

And when you're finished with this book and have absorbed all of the concepts, check out *Robin Williams Design Workshop.* It's a full-color book of more advanced design concepts.

For now, have fun. Lighten up. Don't take all this design stuff too seriously. I guarantee that if you simply follow those four principles, you will be creating dynamic, interesting, organized pages you will be proud of.

Extra tips & tricks

In this chapter we'll look at creating a variety of advertising and promotional pieces for a fictional company called Url's Internet Cafe.* I add lots of other tips and tricks and techniques in this section, but you'll see where the four basic principles apply to every project, no matter how big or small.

This section includes specific tips for designing your business cards, letterhead, envelopes, flyers, newsletters, brochures, direct mail postcards, newspaper ads, and web sites.

---

* There really is an UrlsInternetCafe.com, but the products you see in this chapter are not for sale. Well, they *were* for sale, but the online fulfillment company we used went out of business and our great products disappeared.

Creating a package

One of the most important features of an identity package follows the principle of repetition: there must be some identifying image or style that carries throughout every piece. Take a look at the individual pieces below, all for the Cafe. Name the repetitive elements.

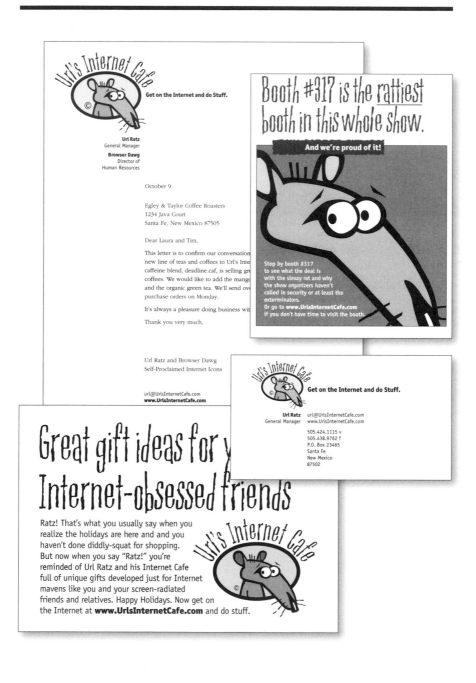

Business cards

If you use a second color, use it sparingly. Most of the time a tiny bit is more effective than throwing the second color all over the card. You get your money's worth with just a splash.

Talk to the print shop about how many copies of the card to set up on one page, and how far apart. Ask if you can send them an Adobe Acrobat PDF file to print from (if you don't know how to make a PDF, you'll find details on Adobe's web site, www.adobe.com). Or buy those perforated, preprinted business cards that you can run through your own office printer (although the perforated edges can give an unprofessional appearance to your business).

Business card size
Standard business card size in the U.S. is **3.5 inches wide by 2 inches tall** (8.5cm x 5.5cm in many other countries). A vertical format, of course, would be 2 inches wide by 3.5 inches tall.

Don't do this!

Url Ratz   General Manager

Url's Internet Cafe
Get on the Internet and do Stuff.

e-mail:
url@UrlsInternetCafe.com
www.UrlsInternetCafe.com

(505) 424-1115 ph.
P.O. Box 23465
Santa Fe, NM 87502

Don't stick things in the corners. The corners don't mind being empty.

Don't use Times, Arial, or Helvetica or your card will always looked dated. Like from the '70s.

Url's Internet Cafe
Get on the Internet and do Stuff.

Url Ratz, General Manager
www.UrlsInternetCafe.com

(505) 424-1115 phone
P.O. Box 23465
Santa Fe, NM 87502

Don't use 12-point type or your card will always look unsophisticated! People can easily read 8-, 9-, or 10-point type. Business cards often use 7-point type. And please don't center your layout unless you can put into words the reason why you need to do so.

Url's Internet Cafe
Get on the Internet and do Stuff.

email: url@UrlsInternetCafe.com
web site: www.UrlsInternetCafe.com

(505) 424-1115 phone   (505) 438-9762 fax
P.O. Box 23465
Santa Fe, NM 87502   Url Ratz,
                    General Manager

Don't feel like you have to fill the entire space on the card. It's okay to have empty space. Look at those professional cards—they always have empty space!

It's unnecessary to have the words "email" and "web site" on your card— it's clear what those particular items are.

Try this . . .

Get on the
Internet
and do Stuff.

Url Ratz
General Manager

url@UrlsInternetCafe.com
www.UrlsInternetCafe.com

505·424·1115 voice
505·438·9762 fax
P.O. Box 23465
Santa Fe, New Mexico 87502

Line things up! Everything on your card should be aligned with something else.

Align baselines.

Align right edges or left edges.

Most of the time a strong flush left or flush right alignment has a much more professional impact than a centered alignment.

Url's Internet Cafe
Get on the Internet and do Stuff.

Url Ratz
General Manager

url@UrlsInternetCafe.com
www.UrlsInternetCafe.com

505.424.1115 v
505.438.9762 f
P.O. Box 23465
Santa Fe, New Mexico
87502

Try using periods, small bullets, or blank spaces instead of parentheses around area codes. It gives your card a cleaner look.

Spell out St., Blvd., Ln., etc. The periods and commas in abbreviations add unnecessary clutter.

If you don't have a fax number, don't type "Phone" before or after your phone number. We know it's your phone number.

Url's Internet Cafe

Url Ratz, Manager
505·424·1115

P.O. Box 23465
Santa Fe
New Mexico 87502
505·438·9762 fax
url@UrlsInternetCafe.com
www.UrlsInternetCafe.com

Tips on designing business cards

Business cards can be a challenge to design because you usually need to pack a lot of information into a small space. And the amount of information you put on a business card has been growing—in addition to the standard address and phone, now you probably need your cell number, fax number, email address, and if you have a web site (which you should), your web address.

Format

Your first choice is whether to work with a **horizontal** format or a **vertical** one. Just because most cards are horizontal doesn't mean they *have* to be. Very often the information fits better in a vertical layout, especially when we have so many pieces of information to include on such a little card. Experiment with both vertical and horizontal layouts, *and choose the one that works best for the information you have on your card.*

Type size

One of the biggest problems with business cards designed by new designers is the type size. It's usually **too big.** Even the 10- or 11-point type we read in books looks horsey on a small card. And 12-point type looks downright dorky. I know it's difficult at first to use 9- or even 8- or 7-point type, but look at the business cards you've collected. Pick out three that look the most professional and sophisticated. They don't use 12-point type.

Keep in mind that a business card is not a book, a brochure, or even an ad—a business card contains information that a client only needs to look at for a couple of seconds. Sometimes the overall, sophisticated effect of the card's design is actually more important than making the type big enough for your great-grandmother to read easily.

Create a consistent image with letterhead and envelope

If you plan to create a letterhead and matching envelopes, you really need to design all three pieces at once. The entire package of business cards, letterhead, and envelopes should present a **consistent image** to clients and customers.

Letterhead and envelopes

Few people look at a company's stationery and think, "This is so beautiful, I'll triple my order," or "This is so ugly, I'll cancel my order" (my friend Laura chose her phone company based on their stationery). But when people see your stationery, they think *something* about you and it's going to be positive or negative, depending on the design and feel of that stationery.

From the quality of the paper you choose, to the design, color, typeface, and the envelope, the implied message should inspire confidence in your business.

The content of your letter will carry substantial weight, but don't overlook the unconscious influence exerted by the letterhead itself.

Be brave! Be bold!

Don't do this!

P.O. Box 23465, Santa Fe, NM, 87502
(505) 424-1115 telephone (505) 438-9762 fax

October 9

Egley and Taylor Coffee Roasters
1234 Java Court
Santa Fe, New Mexico 87505

Dear Laura and Tim,

This letter is to confirm our conversation regarding adding a new line of teas and coffees to
Url's Internet Cafe. The high-caffeine blend, deadline.caf, is selling great, as are the other
coffees. We would like to add the mango-pekoe blend tea and the organic green tea. We'll
send over the contract and purchase orders on Monday.

It's always a pleasure doing business with you!

Thank you very much,

Url Ratz and Browser Dawg
Self-Proclaimed Internet Icons

Don't use a different arrangement on the envelope from what you use on the letterhead and the business card! All three items should look like they belong together.

Url Ratz General Manager

Url's Internet Cafe
Get on the Internet and do Stuff.

e-mail:
url@UrlsInternetCafe.com
www.UrlsInternetCafe.com

(505) 424-1115 ph.
P.O. Box 23465
Santa Fe, NM 87502

Url's Internet Cafe
P.O. Box 23465
Santa Fe, NM 87502

Don't center everything on the page, unless your logo is an obviously centered logo and you must work with it. If you do center, try to be a little more creative with the type, the size, or the placement of the items (that is, even though the items are centered with each other, perhaps they don't have to be directly centered on the page; try placing the entire centered arrangement closer to the left side).

Don't use Times, Arial, or Helvetica.

Just as on your business card, avoid parentheses, abbreviations, and superfluous words that just add clutter.

Try this . . .

Notice how these three pieces have essentially the same layout. Work on all three pieces at the same time to make sure your chosen layout will work in each situation.

Feel free to use type and graphics in a huge way or a small way.

Uncenter the format. Those strong lines of flush left and flush right add strength to your design.

Tips on designing letterhead and envelopes

Your letterhead and envelope should be designed along with your business card. They should all look like they belong together—if you give someone a business card and then later send a letter, you want those pieces to reinforce each other.

Envelope size

The standard business envelope is **9½ x 4⅛ inches.** It's called a #10 envelope. The European size is 110mm x 220mm, and it's called a C4 envelope.

Create a focal point

One element should be **dominant**, and it should be dominant in the same way on both the letterhead and the envelope (and the business card). Please avoid the boring centered-across-the-top layout on the letterhead!

Alignment

Choose one **alignment** for your stationery! Don't center something across the top and then put the rest of the text flush left. Be brave—try flush right down the side with lots of linespacing. Try setting your company name in huge letters across the top. Try placing your logo (or a piece of it) huge and light as a shadow beneath the area where you will type.

On the letterhead, make sure to arrange the elements so when you type the actual letter, the text fits neatly into the design of the stationery.

Second page

If you can afford to make a second page to your stationary, take a **small element** that appears on your first page and use it all by itself on a second page. If you are planning to print, let's say, 1,000 sheets of letterhead, you can usually ask the printer to print something like 800 of the first page and 200 of the second page. Even if you don't plan to print a second page, ask the printer for several hundred blank sheets of the same paper so you have *something* to write longer letters on.

Faxing and copying

If you ever plan to send your letterhead through **fax** or **copy machines,** don't choose a dark paper or one that has lots of speckles in it. Also avoid large areas of dark ink, reverse type, or tiny type that will get lost in the process. If you do a *lot* of faxing, you might want to create two versions of your letterhead—one for print and one for fax.

Flyers

Flyers are great fun to create because you can safely abandon restraint! This is a great place to go wild and really call attention to yourself. As you know, flyers compete with all the other readable junk in the world, especially with other flyers. Often they are posted on a bulletin board with dozens of competing pages that are all trying to grab the attention of passerbys.

A flyer is one of the best places to use fun and different typefaces, and a fun face is one of the best ways to call **attention** to a headline. Don't be a wimp—this is your chance to use one of those really off-the-wall faces you've been lusting after!

And what a great place to experiment with graphics. Just *try* making the graphic image or photograph at least twice the size you originally planned. Or make the headline 400 point instead of 24. Or create a minimalist flyer with one line of 10-point type in the middle of the page and a small block of text at the bottom. Anything out of the ordinary will make people stop and look, and that is 90 percent of your goal.

Don't do this!

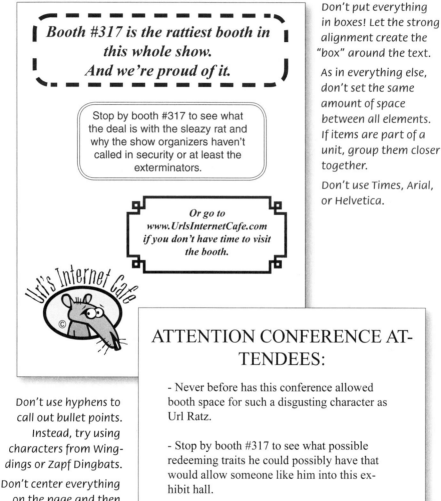

Don't put everything in boxes! Let the strong alignment create the "box" around the text.

As in everything else, don't set the same amount of space between all elements. If items are part of a unit, group them closer together.

Don't use Times, Arial, or Helvetica.

Don't use hyphens to call out bullet points. Instead, try using characters from Wingdings or Zapf Dingbats.

Don't center everything on the page and then put small pieces of text in the corners!

Avoid a gray, boring page—add contrast!

Watch the line breaks—there's no need to break lines at awkward places or to hyphenate unnecessarily.

Try this . . .

Use a huge headline or huge clip art.

Use an interesting typeface in a huge way.

Crop a photograph or clip art into a tall narrow shape; place it along the left edge; align the text flush left.

Or place the art along the right edge and align the text flush right.

Or set the text in several columns, each one flush left.

It's okay to set the body text small on a flyer. If you capture the reader's attention in the first place, she will read the small type.

Tips on designing flyers

The biggest problems with most flyers created by new designers are a lack of contrast and a presentation of information that has no hierarchy. That is, the initial tendency is to make everything large, thinking that it needs to grab someone's attention. But if *everything* is large, then *nothing* can really grab a reader's attention. Use a strong focal point and contrast to organize the information and lead the reader's eye through the page.

Create a focal point

Put one thing on your page that is huge and interesting and **strong.** If you catch their eye with your focal point, they are more likely to read the rest of the text.

Use subheads that contrast

After the focal point, use strong subheads (strong visually, and strong in what it says) so readers can quickly **scan** the flyer to determine the point of the message. If the subheads don't interest them, they're not going to read the copy. But if there are no subheads at all and readers h ave to read every word on the flyer to understand what it's about, they're going to toss it rather than spend the time deciphering the text.

Repetition

Whether your headline uses an ugly typeface, a beautiful face, or an ordinary face in an unusual way, try to pull a little of that same font into the body of the text for **repetition.** Perhaps use just one letter or one word in that same typeface. Use it as your subheads, initial caps, or perhaps as bullets. A strong contrast of typefaces will add interest to your flyer.

Alignment

And remember, choose one alignment! Don't center the headline and then set the body copy flush left, or don't center everything on the page and then stick things in the corners at the bottom. Be strong. Be brave. Try all flush left or flush right.

Newsletters

One of the most important features of a multiple-page publication is consistency, or **repetition.** Every page should look like it belongs to the whole piece. You can do this with color, graphic style, fonts, spatial arrangements, bulleted lists that repeat a formatting style, borders around photographs, captions, etc.

Now, this doesn't mean that everything has to look exactly the same! But (just as in life) if you have a solid foundation you can get away with breaking out of that foundation with glee (and people won't worry about you). Experiment with graphics at a tilt or photographs cropped very wide and narrow and spread across three columns. With that solid foundation, you can set the letter from the president in a special format and it will really stand out.

It's okay to have white space (empty space) in your newsletter. But don't let the white space become "trapped" between other elements. The white space needs to be as organized as the visible elements. Let it be there, and let it flow.

One of the first and most fun things to design in a newsletter is the flag (sometimes called the masthead). This is the piece that sets the tone for the rest of the newsletter.

Don't do this!

Don't be a wimp about your flag (the title of your newsletter on the front page). Tell people who you are!

Don't create a flat, gray newsletter. Use contrasting type where appropriate, create pull-quotes, and add other visually interesting elements to pull the reader's eye into the page.

On the other hand, don't use a different typeface and arrangement for every article. If you create a strong, consistent, underlying structure throughout the newsletter, then you can call attention to a special article by treating it differently.

If everything is different, nothing is special.

Try this . . .

Most people skim through newsletter pages picking out headlines—so make the headlines clear and bold.

You can see the underlying structure of the text here. With the solidity of that structure, the graphics can really juice up the pages by being tilted, enlarged, text-wrapped, etc.

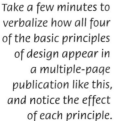

Take a few minutes to verbalize how all four of the basic principles of design appear in a multiple-page publication like this, and notice the effect of each principle.

Tips on designing newsletters

The biggest problems with newsletters seem to be lack of alignment, lack of contrast, and too much Helvetica (Arial is another name for Helvetica).

Alignment

Choose an alignment and stick to it. Trust me—you'll have a stronger and more professional look to your entire newsletter if you maintain that strong edge along the left. And keep everything else aligned. If you use rules (lines), they should begin and end in alignment with something else, like the column edge or column bottom. If your photograph hangs outside the column one-quarter inch, crop it.

You see, if all the elements are neatly aligned, then when appropriate you can freely break out of that alignment with gusto. But don't be a wimp about breaking the alignment—either align the item or don't. Placement that is a *little bit* out of alignment looks like a mistake. If your photo does not fit neatly into the column, then let it break out of the column boldly, not barely.

Paragraph indents

First paragraphs, even after subheads, should not be indented. When you do indent, use the standard typographic indent of one "em" space, which is a space as wide as the point size of your type; that is, if you're using 11-point type, your indent should be 11 points (about two spaces, not five). Use either extra space between paragraphs or an indent, but not both.

Not Helvetica!

If your newsletter looks a little gray and drab, you can instantly juice it up simply by using a strong, heavy, sans serif typeface for your headlines and subheads. Not Helvetica. The Helvetica or Arial that came with your computer isn't bold enough to create a strong contrast. Invest in a sans serif family that includes a heavy black version as well as a light version (such as Eurostile, Formata, Syntax, Frutiger, or Myriad). Use that heavy black for your headlines and pull-quotes and you'll be amazed at the difference.

Readable body copy

For best readability, avoid using a sans serif for the body copy. Try a classic oldstyle serif face (such as Garamond, Jenson, Caslon, Minion, or Palatino), or a lightweight slab serif (such as Clarendon, Bookman, Kepler, or New Century Schoolbook). What you're reading right now is Warnock Pro Light from Adobe.

Brochures

Brochures are a quick and inexpensive way to get the word out about your brand new homemade-pie business, school fundraiser, or upcoming scavenger hunt. Dynamic, well-designed brochures can be "eye candy" for readers, drawing them in and educating them in a delightful and painless way.

Armed with the basic design principles, you can create eye-grabbing brochures of your own. The tips on the next couple of pages will help.

Before you sit down to design the brochure, fold a piece of paper into the intended shape and make notes on each flap. Pretend you just found it—in what order do you read the panels?

Keep in mind the order in which the panels of a brochure are presented to the reader as they open it. For instance, when a reader opens the front cover, they should not be confronted with the copyright and contact information.

The fold measurements are not the same on the front as they are on the back! After you fold your paper sample, measure from left to right on front and back. **Do not simply divide 11 inches into thirds—** it won't work.

A brochure can be your number-one marketing tool.

It's important to be aware of the folds; you don't want important information disappearing into the creases! **If you have a strong alignment for the text** on each panel of the brochure, however, feel free to let the graphics cross over the space between the columns of text (the **gutter**) and into the fold. See the example on page 107.

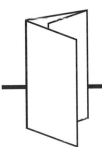

The three-fold style shown to the left is by far the most commonly seen for brochures (because it works so well for letter-sized paper), but there are lots of other fold options available. Check with your print shop.

The brochure examples on the following pages are set up for a standard, 8.5 x 11-inch, three-fold brochure like this one.

Don't do this!

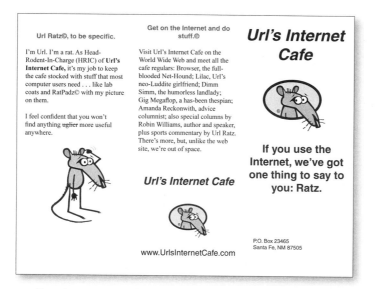

Don't set items centered and flush left on the cover (or inside)!
Pick one alignment. Please.

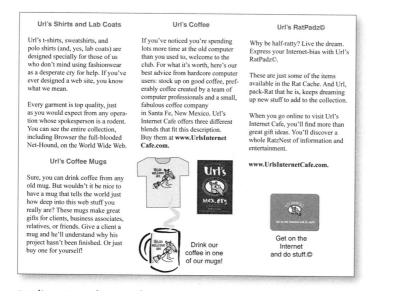

Don't use 12-point type for your body copy. Besides looking unsophisticated, 12-point in most typefaces is too large for the column width in a standard three-fold brochure.

Don't set the copy too close to the fold. Remember that you're going to fold the paper down the middle of the column gutter, so allow more room between columns in a brochure than you would in a newsletter.

Try this . . .

Which panel will the reader see first? second? This brochure is designed to draw the reader in little by little.

After the initial powerful greeting on the cover panel, the reader gets an introduction to the mascot for the company on the next panel, then finally opens to the inside of the brochure.

Notice how contrast of color and size are used here.

Play with the graphic images in your brochure—make them bigger, overlap them, wrap text around them, tilt them. You can do all this if your text presents a solid, aligned base.

See how the only things that cross the gutter (the fold area in between text blocks) are pieces of art? Graphics don't get lost in the fold.

Tips on designing brochures

Brochures created by new designers have many of the same problems as newsletters: lack of contrast, lack of alignment, and too much Helvetica/Arial. Here's a quick summary of how the principle elements of design can be applied to that brochure you're working on.

Contrast

As in any other design project, contrast not only adds visual interest to a page so a reader's eye is drawn in, but it also helps create the hierarchy of information so the reader can scan the important points and understand what the brochure is about. Use contrast in the typefaces, rules, colors, spacing, size of elements, etc. Remember that the only way contrast is effective is if it's strong—if two elements are not exactly the same, make sure they are **very** different. Otherwise it looks like a mistake. Don't be a wimp.

Repetition

Repeat various elements in the design to create a **unified look** to the piece. You might repeat colors, typefaces, rules, spatial arrangements, bullets, etc.

Alignment

I keep repeating myself about this alignment stuff, but it's important, and the lack of it is consistently a problem. **Strong, sharp edges** create a strong, sharp impression. A combination of alignments (using centered, flush left, and flush right in one piece) usually creates a sloppy, weak impression.

Occasionally, you may want to intentionally break out of the alignment (as I did on page 107); **this will only work if you have other strong alignments** to contrast with the breakout.

Proximity

Proximity, **grouping** similar items close together, is especially important in a project such as a brochure where you have a variety of subtopics within one main topic. How close and how far away items are from each other communicates the relationships of the items.

To create the spatial arrangements effectively, **you must know how to use your software** to create space between the paragraphs (space before or space after) instead of hitting the Enter or Return key twice. Two Returns between paragraphs creates a larger gap than you need, forcing items apart that should be close together. Two Returns also creates the same amount of space *above* a headline or subhead as there is *below* the head (which you don't want), and it separates bulleted items that should be closer together. Learn that software!

Postcards

Because they're so visual and so immediate—no envelopes to fuss with, no paper cuts—postcards are a great way to grab attention. And for these same reasons, an ugly or boring postcard is a waste of everybody's time.

So, to avoid waste, remember the following:

Be different. Oversized or oddly shaped postcards will stand out from that crowd in the mailbox.

Think "series." A single postcard makes one impression; just think what a series of several could do!

Be specific. Tell the recipient exactly how they'll benefit (and what they need to do to get that benefit).

Keep it brief. Use the front of the postcard for a short and attention-getting message. Put less important details on the back.

If possible, use color. Besides being fun to work with, color attracts the eye and draws interest.

17th Annual Invitational

Neighborhood

Cleanup

& Bake Sale

Saturday, May 20
8 a.m. – 12 noon
Sponsored by
Url's Internet Cafe

Don't forget: white space is a design element, too!

Don't do this!

Great gift ideas for your Internet-obsessed friends

RATZ! THAT'S WHAT YOU USUALLY SAY WHEN YOU REALIZE THE HOLIDAYS ARE HERE AND YOU HAVEN'T DONE DIDDLY-SQUAT FOR SHOPPING. BUT NOW WHEN YOU SAY "RATZ!" YOU'RE REMINDED OF URL RATZ AND HIS INTERNET CAFE FULL OF UNIQUE GIFTS DEVELOPED JUST FOR INTERNET MAVENS LIKE YOU AND YOUR SCREEN-RADIATED FRIENDS AND RELATIVES. HAPPY HOLIDAYS. NOW GET ON THE INTERNET AT WWW.URLSINTERNETCAFE.COM AND DO STUFF.

What's wrong with this headline?

Don't use 12-point Helvetica, Arial, or Times.

Don't set information in all caps because it is so difficult to read that no one will read it. They didn't ask for the card in the first place, did they?

Use contrast and spatial relationships to communicate a message clearly.

Great GIFT IDEAS for your Internet-obsessed friends

Ratz! That's what you usually say when you realize the holidays are here and you haven't done diddly-squat for shopping. But now when you say "Ratz!" you're reminded of Url Ratz and his Internet Cafe full of unique gifts developed just for Internet mavens like you and your screen-radiated friends and relatives.

Now get on the Internet at www.urlsinternetCafe.com and do stuff.

Happy Holidays.

The guidelines for business cards (pages 89–92) also apply to postcards: don't stick things in the corners; don't think you have to fill the space; don't make everything the same size or almost the same size.

Try this . . .

Great gift ideas for your Internet-obsessed friends

Ratz! That's what you usually say when you realize the holidays are here and you haven't done diddly-squat for shopping. But now when you say "Ratz!" you're reminded of Url Ratz and his Internet Cafe full of **unique gifts** developed just for Internet mavens like you and your screen-radiated friends and relatives. Happy Holidays.

Now get on the Internet at **www.UrlsInternetCafe.com** and do stuff.

Try an odd size postcard, such as tall and narrow, short and fat, oversized, or a fold-over card.

Just be sure to take your intended size and paper to the post office and make sure it fits regulations before you print it! And verify the cost of postage for an odd-sized card.

As in any piece where you need to get someone's attention instantly, create a hierarchy of information so the reader can scan the card and make a quick decision as to whether they want to read the rest of it or not.

Great gift ideas for your Internet-obsessed friends

Ratz© Thats what you usually say when you realize the holidays are here and and you haven't done diddly-squat for shopping. But now when you say "Ratz©" you're reminded of Url Ratz and his Internet Cafe full of unique gifts developed just for Internet mavens like you and your screen-radiated friends and relatives. Happy Holidays. Now get on the Internet at **www.UrlsInternetCafe.com** and do stuff.

Tips on designing postcards

You only have a split second to capture someone's attention with an unsolicited postcard that arrives in the mail. No matter how great your copy, if the design of the card does not attract their attention, they won't read your copy.

What's your point?

Your first decision is to determine what sort of effect you want to achieve. Do you want readers to think it is an expensive, exclusive offer? Then your postcard had better look as expensive and professional as the product. Do you want readers to feel like they're getting a great bargain? Then your postcard shouldn't be too slick. Discount places spend extra money to make their stores look like they contain bargains. It's not an accident that Saks Fifth Avenue has a different look—from the parking lot to the restrooms—than does Kmart, and it doesn't mean that Kmart spent less on decor than did Saks. Each look serves a distinct and definite purpose and reaches out toward a specific market.

Grab their attention

The same design guidelines apply to direct-mail postcards as to anything else: contrast, repetition, alignment, and proximity. But with this kind of postcard, you have very little time to induce recipients into reading it. **Be brave** with bright colors, either in the ink or the card stock. Use striking graphics — there's plenty of great and inexpensive clip art you can use in all sorts of creative ways.

Contrast

Contrast is probably your best friend in a direct-mail postcard. The headline should be in strong contrast to the rest of the text, the colors should use strong contrast to each other and to the color of the paper stock. And don't forget that **white space** creates contrast!

Newspaper ads

A well-designed newspaper ad can work wonders for an advertiser; however, looking good is not all it takes to be successful in newsprint. Here are a few hints that will help even the sexiest ad rake in results:

White space! Take note of yourself next time you scan the newspaper. Which ads do your eyes naturally land on, and which ads do you actually read? I'll bet you see and read at least the headlines of the ads that have more white space.

Be clever. There's nothing that can compete with a clever headline. Not even good design. (But with both, the possibilities multiply!)

Be clear. Once your catchy headline has garnered some attention, your ad should specifically tell readers what to do (and give them the means to do so, i.e. phone number, email address, web address, etc.).

Be brief. Your ad is not the place to put your life story. Keep the copy simple and to the point.

Use color when you can. It always attracts the eye, particularly when surrounded by a sea of gray text.

Summertime Snowball Sale

Url saved up all winter so you could bring a little cold weather home this summer.

Snowballs 2/$5   All day Saturday, July 25   9-6   Url's Internet Cafe

Ads don't have to scream to be effective.

Don't do this!

THIS IS THE TECHNOLOGY AGE. LAB COATS FOR SALE.

You could also use a t-shirt that tells your clients the Internet facts of life. And coffees blended specifically for web surfers.

You'll need matching mugs for the coffee and most likely you'll want original RatPadz© to replace those clunky old mouse pads you have just lying around the office.

Did we mention polo shirts, caps, gift boxes, and do-rags? Prepare yourself for the Technology Age: visit Url's Internet Cafe for great gift ides and a cafe full of educational, fun stuff.

www.UrlsInternetCafe.com

If your headline doesn't grab their attention, they won't read your body copy no matter how big you set it. (If you get rid of the caps, your headline can be set much larger.)

Don't make all the text the same size. Call out your headline, but once you catch the reader's eye and mind with your headline, they will read the rest of the text, even if it's 9-point type.

WOULD YOU BUY A LAB COAT FROM AN UGLY RAT?

You may not think so now, but just wait 'til you see the lab coats, t-shirts, caps, polo shirts, special coffees, teas, mugs, RatPadz©, and other great gift ideas at Url's Internet Cafe.

But people don't come here just to shop. It's a cafe where just hangin' out is an art form. And when that sudden impulse to buy a lab coat hits, we've got 'em right here. So, if you think he's a sleazy, ugly rat, you're right. But come on, how many handsome lab coat salesmen do you know?

www.UrlsInternetCafe.com
P.O. Box 23465
Santa Fe, NM 87505
(505) 424-1115

Don't cram the space full! I know you paid for it, but white space is just as valuable and well worth the money.

Unless your ad offers valuable, free information that a reader really wants to know and can't get anywhere else, don't stuff it. Let there be white space.

Try this . . .

White space is good. The trick about white space is that it needs to be organized. In the first ad on the opposite page, there is just as much white space as there is in this ad to the right, but it's sprawled all over the place.

Organize the white space just as consciously as you organize the information.

As with any other design project, use contrast, repetition, alignment, and proximity. Can you name where each of those concepts have been used in these ads?

Tips on designing newspaper ads

One of the biggest problems with newspaper ads is crowding. Many clients and businesses who are paying for a newspaper ad feel they need to fill every particle of space because it costs money.

Contrast

With a newspaper ad, you need contrast not only in the advertisement itself, but also between the ad and the rest of the newspaper page that it's placed on. In this kind of ad, the best way to create contrast is with white space. Newspaper pages tend to be completely full of stuff and very busy. An ad that has lots of white space within it stands out on the page, and a reader's eye can't help but be drawn to it. Experiment with yourself. Open a newspaper page (or a phone book page) and scan it. I guarantee that if there is white space on that page, your eyes will go to it. They go there because white space provides a strong contrast on a full, busy page.

Once you have white space, your headline doesn't need to be in a big, fat, typeface screaming to compete with everything else. You can actually get away with a beautiful script or a classy oldstyle instead of a heavy face.

Type choices

Newsprint is porous, coarse paper, and the ink spreads on it. So don't use a typeface that has small, delicate serifs or very thin lines that will thicken when printed, unless you are setting the type large enough that the serifs and strokes will hold up.

Reverse type

Avoid reverse type (white type on a dark background) if possible, but if you must have it, make sure you use a good solid typeface with no thin lines that will fill in when the ink spreads. As always when setting type in reverse, use a point size a wee bit larger and bolder than you would if it was not reversed because the optical illusion makes reverse type appear smaller and thinner.

Web sites

While the same four basic principles I've mentioned over and over in this book (contrast, repetition, alignment, proximity) also apply to web design, **repetition** is one of the most important for a web site. The other three principles help the pages look good and make sense, but repetition lets your visitors know whether they're still in the same web site. You should have a consistent navigation system and graphic style so your visitors always know they are in the same web site. Repeating a color scheme, the same typefaces, buttons, or similar-style graphic elements placed in the same position on each page will do the trick.

Designing a web site is quite a bit different from designing printed pieces. If you're brand-new to web design and want to learn how to get started, you really should check out *The Non-Designer's Web Book.* Once you've mastered the basics in that book, look into *Robin Williams Web Design Workshop.*

Your web site should be inviting and easy to move around in. This site is clean and simple. Google.com is a great example of a fabulous, useful, yet clean and simple site.

Don't do this!

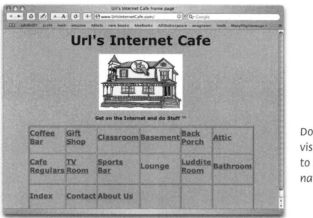

Don't make
visitors scroll
to see the
navigation links!

Don't use the default blue color for your text or graphic links.
It's a sure sign of an amateur page.

Don't make text links within big, dorky, table cells with the
borders turned on.

Don't make a link on the home page to every page in your site.
Group related pages together.

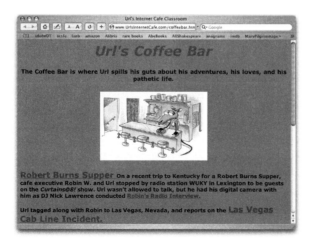

Don't let text
bump up against
the left edge of the
browser window.

Don't use a fluorescent background color, especially with
fluorescent type!

Don't make the visitor scroll sideways!! Keep your page
within the 800-pixel width maximum. Especially don't
make a table that is wider than 600 pixels or people will be
very mad at you when they try to print your page.

Try this . . .

Keep your entry page and your home page within a framework of 800 pixels wide by 600 pixels deep. A visitor should not have to scroll on a home page to find the links!

Absence of the bad features of web design takes you a long way toward good web design.

Take a look at Peachpit.com or Adobe.com. Name at least five things that provide the visitor with a consistent look-and-feel so the visitor always knows, no matter what page they are on, that they are in the Adobe site.

Put into words exactly what makes the difference between the examples on these two pages. Stating the design features—good and bad—out loud, naming them, helps you design better.

Tips on designing web pages

Two of the most important factors in good web design are **repetition and clarity.** A visitor should never have to figure out how to use your navigation system, where they are in the site, or whether they are still in your web site or have jumped somewhere else.

Repetition

Repeat certain visual elements on every page in your web site. This not only lets the visitor know they are still at your site, but also provides unity and continuity, intrinsic features of any good design.

Once you get to content pages, the visitor should find the navigation in the same place, in the same order, with the same graphics. Not only does this make it easy for the visitor to find their way through your site, but it provides a unifying factor to the collection of pages.

Readability

One of the most unreadable places to read text is on a monitor, whether it's television, video, or computer. So we need to make a few adjustments to the text on web pages to make sure it's as easy to read as possible.

Use **shorter line lengths** than you might use on paper. The body copy should never run the entire width of the web page, which means you must put the text in a table (or at least use a block indent, which indents the text from both the left and right sides). But don't use such short line lengths that you break up the phrasing of the sentences too much.

If you are specifying the text to appear in a certain typeface (if you're not, ignore this), typically Helvetica or Arial and Times or Times Roman, please specify Geneva in front of Helvetica, and New York in front of Times. This will make the text on Macintoshes appear much so much cleaner and easier to read. (If you use a Mac, set your default font to New York instead of Times, and you will be amazed at how much easier it is to read web pages. Change it back to Times before you print a page.) Verdana is found on all operating systems updated within the past few years, and it's an excellent choice for body copy on the web.

Designing with TYPE

The second half of this book
deals specifically with type,
since type is what design
is all about, yes?
This section particularly
addresses the problem
of combining more than one
typeface on the page.

Although I focus
on the aesthetics of type,
never forget
that your purpose is
communication.
The type should never
inhibit the communication.

What type shall I use?

The gods refuse

to answer.

They refuse

because

they

do not

know.

W.A. Dwiggins

Type *(& Life)*

Type is the basic building block of any printed page. Often it is irresistibly compelling and sometimes absolutely imperative to design a page with more than one typeface on it. But how do you know which typefaces work effectively together?

In Life, when there is more than one of anything, a dynamic relationship is established. In Type, there is usually more than one element on a page—even a document of plain body copy typically has heads or subheads or at least page numbers on it. Within these dynamics on the page (or in life), a relationship is established that is either concordant, conflicting, or contrasting.

A **concordant** relationship occurs when you use only one type family without much variety in style, size, weight, and so on. It is easy to keep the page harmonious, and the arrangement tends to appear quiet and rather sedate or formal—sometimes downright dull.

A **conflicting** relationship occurs when you combine typefaces that are *similar* in style, size, weight, and so on. The similarities are disturbing because the visual attractions are not the same (concordant), but neither are they different (contrasting), so they conflict.

A **contrasting** relationship occurs when you combine separate typefaces and elements that are clearly distinct from each other. The visually appealing and exciting designs that attract your attention typically have a lot of contrast built in, and the contrasts are emphasized.

Most designers tend to wing it when combining more than one typeface on a page. You might have a sense that one face needs to be larger or an element needs to be bolder. However, when you can recognize and *name the contrasts*, you have power over them—you can then get to the root of the conflicting problem faster and find more interesting solutions. And *that* is the point of this section.

Concord

A design is concordant when you choose to use just one face and the other elements on the page have the same qualities as that typeface. Perhaps you use some of the italic version, and perhaps a larger size for a heading, and maybe a graphic or several ornaments—but the basic impression is still concordant.

Most concordant designs tend to be rather calm and formal. This does not mean concord is undesirable—just be aware of the impression you give by using elements that are all in concord with each other.

Life's but a walking shadow, a poor player

that struts and frets his hour upon the stage,

and then is heard no more; it is a tale

told by an idiot, *full of sound and fury,*

signifying nothing.

This concordant example uses Cochin. The first letter is larger and there is some italic type (Cochin Italic), but the entire piece is rather subdued.

The heavy typeface combines well with the heavy border. Even the line for writing on is a bit heavy.

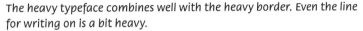

The typeface, the thin border, and the delicate ornaments all give the same style impression.

Look familiar? Lots of folks play it safe with their wedding invitations by using the principle of concord.

Conflict

A design is in conflict when you set two or more typefaces on the same page that are *similar*—not really different and not really the same. I have seen countless students trying to match a typeface with one on the page, looking for a face that "looks similar." Wrong. When you put two faces together that look too much alike without really being so, most of the time it looks like a mistake. *The problem is in the similarities.*

Concord is a solid and useful concept; **conflict** should be avoided.

Life's but a walking shadow, a poor player

that struts and frets his hour upon the stage,

and then is heard no more; it is a tale

told by an idiot, full of sound and fury,

signifying nothing.

As you read this example, what happens when you get to the phrase, "full of sound and fury"? Do you wonder why it's in another type-face? Do you wonder if perhaps it's a mistake? Does it make you twitch? Does the large initial letter look like it is supposed to be there?

What's up?

My name is _____

My theme song is _____

When I grow up I want to be _____

Look particularly at the "a," the "t," and the "s" in the headline and the other lines. They are similar but not the same. The border is not the same visual weight as the type or the lines, nor are they in strong contrast. There is too much conflict in this little piece.

You are cordially invited

to share in our

wedding celebration

Popeye & Olive Oyl

April 1

3 o'clock in the afternoon

Berkeley Square

This small invitation uses two different scripts—they have many similarities with each other, but they are not the same and they are not different.

The ornaments have the same type of conflict. The piece looks a bit cluttered.

Contrast

There is no quality in this world that is not what it is merely by contrast. Nothing exists in itself. —Herman Melville

Now this is the fun part. Creating concord is pretty easy, and creating conflict is easy but undesirable. Creating contrast is just fun.

Strong contrast attracts our eyes, as you learned in the previous section about design. One of the most effective, simplest, and satisfying ways to add contrast to a design is with type.

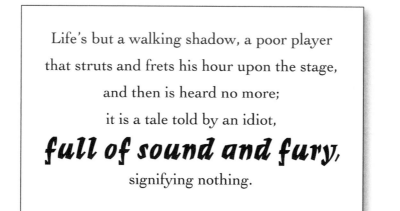

Life's but a walking shadow, a poor player
that struts and frets his hour upon the stage,
and then is heard no more;
it is a tale told by an idiot,
full of sound and fury,
signifying nothing.

In this example it's very clear that the phrase "full of sound and fury" is supposed to be in another typeface. The entire piece of prose has a more exciting visual attraction and a greater energy due to the contrast of type.

Hello!

My name is _____

My theme song is _____

When I grow up I want to be _____

Now the contrast between the typefaces is clear (they are actually in the same family: Antique Olive)—the very bold face contrasts the very light face. The line weights of the border and writing lines also have a clear distinction.

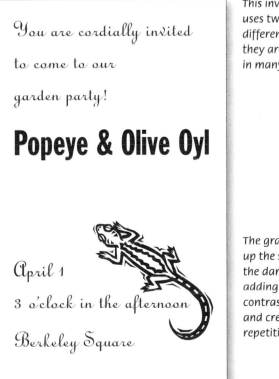

You are cordially invited

to come to our

garden party!

Popeye & Olive Oyl

April 1

3 o'clock in the afternoon

Berkeley Square

This invitation uses two very different faces—they are different in many ways.

The graphic picks up the strength of the dark typeface, adding another contrast to the script and creating a repetitive touch.

Summary

Contrast is not just for the aesthetic look of the piece. It is intrinsically tied in with the organization and clarity of the information on the page. Never forget that your point is to communicate. Combining different typefaces should enhance the communication, not confuse it.

There are six clear and distinct ways to contrast type: size, weight, structure, form, direction, and color. The rest of this book talks about each of these contrasts in turn.

Although I elaborate on each of the contrasts one at a time, rarely is one contrast effective. Most often you will strengthen the effect by combining and emphasizing the differences.

If you have trouble seeing what is wrong with a combination of typefaces, don't look for what is *different* between the faces—look for what is *similar.* It is the similarities that are causing the problem.

The one rule to follow when contrasting type is this: *don't be a wimp!*

But...

Before we get to the ways to contrast, you need to have a familiarity with the categories of type. Spend a couple of minutes with each page in the next chapter, noting the similarities that unify a category of type. Then try to find a couple of examples of that kind of type before you move on to the next category. Look in magazines, books, on packages, anything printed. Believe me, taking a few moments to do this will make everything sink in so much faster and deeper!

Categories of type

There are many thousands of different typefaces available right now, and many more being created every day. Most faces, though, can be dropped into one of the six categories mentioned below. Before you try to become conscious of the *contrasts* in type, you should become aware of the *similarities* between broad groups of type designs, because it is the *similarities* that cause the conflicts in type combinations. The purpose of this chapter is to make you more aware of the details of letterforms. In the next chapter I'll launch into combining them.

Of course, you will find hundreds of faces that don't fit neatly into any category. We could make several hundred different categories for the varieties in type — don't worry about it. The point is just to start looking at type more closely and clearly.

I focus on these six groups:

Oldstyle

Modern

Slab serif

Sans serif

Script

Decorative

Oldstyle

Typefaces created in the **oldstyle** category are based on the handlettering of scribes—you can imagine a wedge-tipped pen held in the hand. Oldstyles always have serifs (see the call-out below) and the serifs of lowercase letters are always at an angle (the angle of the pen). Because of that pen, all the curved strokes in the letterforms have a transition from thick to thin, technically called the "thick/thin transition." This contrast in the stroke is relatively moderate, meaning it goes from kind-of-thin to kind-of-thicker. If you draw a line through the thinnest parts of the curved strokes, the line is diagonal. This is called the *stress*—oldstyle type has a diagonal stress.

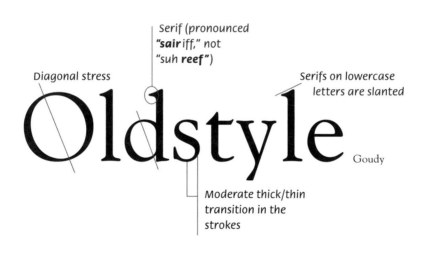

Serif (pronounced **"sair** iff," not "suh **reef")**

Diagonal stress

Serifs on lowercase letters are slanted

Oldstyle

Goudy

Moderate thick/thin transition in the strokes

Goudy   Palatino   Times

Baskerville   Garamond

Do these faces all look pretty much the same to you? Don't worry—they look the same to everyone who hasn't studied typography. Their "invisibility" is exactly what makes oldstyles the best type group for extensive amounts of body copy. There are rarely any distinguishing characteristics that get in the way of reading; they don't call attention to themselves. If you're setting lots of type that you want people to actually read, choose an oldstyle.

Modern

As history marched on, the structure of type changed. Type has trends and succumbs to lifestyle and cultural changes, just like hairdos, clothes, architecture, or language. In the 1700s, smoother paper, more sophisticated printing techniques, and a general increase in mechanical devices led to type becoming more mechanical also. New typefaces no longer followed the pen in hand. Modern typefaces have serifs, but the serifs are now horizontal instead of slanted, and they are very thin. Like a steel bridge, the structure is severe, with a radical thick/thin transition, or contrast, in the strokes. There is no evidence of the slant of the pen; the stress is perfectly vertical. Moderns tend to have a cold, elegant look.

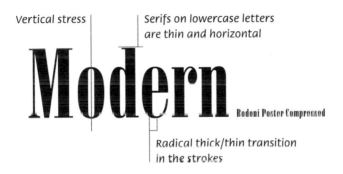

Vertical stress | Serifs on lowercase letters are thin and horizontal

Bodoni Poster Compressed

Radical thick/thin transition in the strokes

Bodoni **Times Bold** **Onyx**

Fenice, Ultra **Walbaum**

Modern typefaces have a striking appearance, especially when set very large. Because of their strong thick/thin transitions, most moderns are not good choices for extended amounts of body copy. The thin lines almost disappear, the thick lines are prominent, and the effect on the page is called "dazzling."

Slab serif

Along with the industrial revolution came a new concept: advertising. At first, advertisers took modern typefaces and made the thicks thicker. You've seen posters with type like that—from a distance, all you see are vertical lines, like a fence. The obvious solution to this problem was to thicken the entire letterform. Slab serifs have little or no thick/thin transition.

This category of type is sometimes called Clarendon, because the typeface Clarendon (shown below) is the epitome of this style. They are also called Egyptian because they became popular during the Egyptomania phase of Western civilization; many typefaces in this category were given Egyptian names so they would sell (Memphis, Cairo, Scarab).

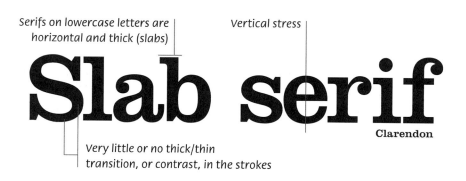

Serifs on lowercase letters are horizontal and thick (slabs)

Vertical stress

Slab serif

Clarendon

Very little or no thick/thin transition, or contrast, in the strokes

Clarendon   Memphis

Memphis Extra Bold

New Century Schoolbook

Many of the slab serifs that have a slight thick/thin contrast (such as Clarendon or New Century Schoolbook) are very high on the readability scale, meaning they can easily be used in extensive text. They present an overall darker page than oldstyles, though, because their strokes are thicker and relatively monoweight. Slab serifs are often used in children's books because of their clean, straightforward look.

Sans serif

The word "sans" means "without" (in French), so sans serif typefaces are those without serifs on the ends of the strokes. The idea of removing the serifs was a rather late development in the evolution of type and didn't become wildly successful until the early part of the twentieth century.

Sans serif typefaces are almost always "monoweight," meaning there is virtually no visible thick/thin transition in the strokes; the letterforms are the same thickness all the way around.

Also see the following page for important sans serif information.

No serifs anywhere

No thick/thin transition in the strokes

No stress because there's no thick/thin

Franklin Gothic

Antique Olive **Formata**

Folio **Franklin Gothic**

Futura, Condensed Syntax

If the only sans serifs you have in your font library are Helvetica and Avant Garde, the best thing you could do for your pages is invest in a sans serif family that includes a strong, heavy, black face. Each of the families above has a wide variety of weights, from light to extra black. With that one investment, you will be amazed at how your options increase for creating eye-catching pages.

Most sans serifs are monoweight, as shown on the preceding page. A very few, however, have a slight thick/thin transition. Below is an example of a sans serif with a stress, called Optima. Faces like Optima are very difficult to combine on a page with other type—they have similarities with serif faces in the thick/thin strokes, and they have similarities with sans serifs in the lack of serifs. Be very careful when working with a sans like this.

Sans serif Optima

Optima is an exceptionally beautiful typeface, but you must be very careful about combining it with other faces. Notice its thick/thin strokes. It has the classic grace of an oldstyle, but with the serifs removed.

Ever notice that
'What the heck'
is always
the right decision?

—*Nancy Davis*

Here you see Optima combined with Spumoni. Spumoni's spunky informality is a nice contrast with Optima's classic grace.

Script

The script category includes all those typefaces that appear to have been handlettered with a calligraphy pen or brush, or sometimes with a pencil or technical pen. This category could easily be broken down into scripts that connect, scripts that don't connect, scripts that look like hand printing, scripts that emulate traditional calligraphic styles, and so on. But for our purposes we are going to lump them all into one pot.

Arid   Shelley Volante   Legacy

Cascade *Linoscript* Zapf Chancery

Scripts are like cheesecake—they should be used sparingly so nobody gets sick. The fancy ones, of course, should never be set as long blocks of text and *never* as all caps. But scripts can be particularly stunning when set very large—don't be a wimp!

Carpe Diem

Decorative

Decorative fonts are easy to identify—if the thought of reading an entire book in that font makes you wanna throw up, you can probably put it in the decorative pot. Decorative fonts are great—they're fun, distinctive, easy to use, oftentimes cheaper, and there is a font for any whim you wish to express. Of course, simply because they *are* so distinctive, their powerful use is limited.

When using a decorative typeface, go beyond what you think of as its initial impression. For instance, if Improv strikes you as informal, try using it in a more formal situation and see what happens. If you think Juniper carries a Wild West flavor, try it in a corporate setting or a flower shop and see what happens. Depending on how you use them, decoratives can carry obvious emotions, or you can manipulate them into carrying connotations very different from your first impression. But that is a topic for another book.

Wisdom sometimes benefits from the use of decorative fonts.

Be conscious

To use type effectively, you have to be conscious. By that I mean you must keep your eyes open, you must notice details, you must try to state the problem in words. Or when you see something that appeals to you strongly, put into words *why* it appeals to you.

Spend a few minutes and look through a magazine. Try to categorize the typefaces you see. Many of them won't fit neatly into a single pot, but that's okay—choose the category that seems the closest. The point is that you are looking more closely at letterforms, which is absolutely critical if you are going to combine them effectively.

Little Quiz #3: Categories of type

Draw lines to match the category with the typeface!

Oldstyle   **AT THE RODEO**

Modern   **High Society**

Slab serif   *Too Sassy for Words*

Sans serif   As I remember, Adam

Script   The enigma continues

Decorative   *It's your attitude*

Little Quiz #4: Thick/thin transitions

Do the following typefaces have:

A moderate thick/thin transitions

B radical thick/thin transitions

C no (or negligible) thick/thin transitions

Giggle

A B C

Jiggle

A B C

Diggle

A B C

Piggle

A B C

Higgle

A B C

Wiggle

A B C

Little Quiz #5: Serifs

Do the lowercase letters in the examples below have:

A thin, horizontal serifs

B thick, slabby [hint] horizontal serifs

C no serifs

D slanted serifs

Diggle
A B C D

Riggle
A B C D

Figgle
A B C D

Biggle
A B C D

Miggle
A B C D

Tiggle
A B C D

Notice the huge differences between all the "g" letters! Too much fun.

Summary

I can't stress enough how important it is that you become conscious of these broad categories of type. As you work through the next chapter, it will become clearer *why* this is important.

A simple exercise to continually hone your visual skills is to collect samples of the categories. Cut them out of any printed material you can find. Do you see any patterns developing within a broad category? Go ahead and make subsets, such as oldstyle typefaces that have small x-heights and tall descenders (see the example below). Or scripts that are really more like hand printing than cursive handwriting. Or extended faces and condensed faces (see below). It is this visual awareness of the letterforms that will give you the power to create interesting, provocative, and effective type combinations.

Bernhard xq

30 point

Ascenders *are the parts of letters that are taller than the x-height.*

*The **x-height** is the height of the main body of the lowercase letters.*

Descenders *are the parts of letters that are below the **baseline** (the invisible line on which the type sits).*

Notice the x-height of Bernhard as compared to Eurostile, below. Look at the x-height in relation to the ascenders. Bernhard has an unusually small x-height and unusually tall ascenders. Most sans serifs have large x-heights. Start noticing those kinds of details.

Eurostile Bold 18 point

Eurostile Bold Extended

Eurostile Bold Condensed

Extended typefaces look stretched out; condensed typefaces appear to be squished. Both are appropriate in certain circumstances.

Type contrasts

This chapter focuses on the topic of combining typefaces. The following pages describe the various ways type can be contrasted. Each page shows specific examples, and at the end of this section are examples using these principles of contrasting type on your pages. Type contrast is not only for the aesthetic appeal, but also to enhance the communication.

A reader should never have to try to figure out what is happening on the page—the focus, the organization of material, the purpose, the flow of information, all should be recognized instantly with a single glance. And along the way, it doesn't hurt to make it beautiful!

These are the contrasts I discuss:

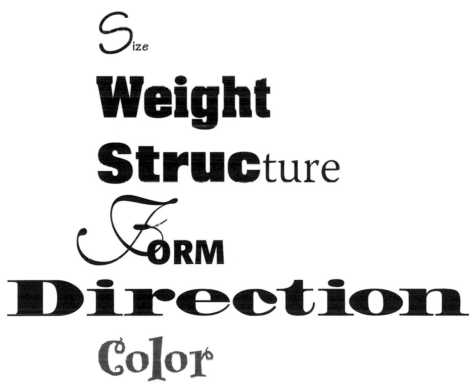

Size

Weight

Structure

Form

Direction

Color

In which category
of type does this
face belong?

A contrast of size is fairly obvious: big type versus little type. To make a contrast of size work effectively, though, *don't be a wimp.* You cannot contrast 12-point type with 14-point type; most of the time they will simply conflict. You cannot contrast 65-point type with 72-point type. If you're going to contrast two typographic elements through their size, *then do it.* Make it obvious—don't let people think it's a mistake.

HEY, SHE'S CALLING YOU A LITTLE

Decide on the typographic element that you want seen as a focus. Emphasize it with contrasts.

A N O T H E R

Volume 1 ■ Number 1   January ■ 2008

If other typographic elements have to be there, but they aren't really that important to the general reading public, make them small. Who cares what the volume number is? If someone does care, it can still be read. It's okay not to set it in 12-point type!

A contrast of size does not always mean you must make the type large—it just means there should be a contrast. For instance, when you see a small line of type alone on a large newspaper page, you are compelled to read it, right? An important part of what compells you is the contrast of very small type on that large page.

If you came across this full page in a newspaper, would you read that small type in the middle? Contrast does that.

Sometimes the contrast of big over little can be overwhelming, overpowering the smaller type. Use that to your advantage. Who wants to notice the word "incorporated" anyway? Although it's small, it's certainly not invisible so it's there for those who need it.

I recommend over and over again not to use all caps. You probably use all caps sometimes to make the type larger, yes? Ironically, when type is set in all caps it can be up to twice as long as the same words set in lowercase, so you have to make the point size smaller. If you make the text lowercase, you can actually set it in a much larger point size, plus it's more readable.

This title is in 18-point type. That's the largest size I can use in this space with all caps.

By making the title lowercase, I could enlarge it to 24-point type, plus still have room to make it heavier.

Use a contrast of size in unusual and provocative ways. Many of our typographic symbols, such as numbers, ampersands, or quotation marks, are very beautiful when set extremely large. Use them as decorative elements in a headline or a pull quote, or as repetitive elements throughout a publication.

The sound & the fury

An unusual contrast of size can become a graphic element in itself—handy if you are limited in the graphics available for a project.

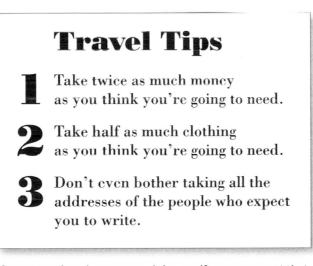

Travel Tips

1 Take twice as much money as you think you're going to need.

2 Take half as much clothing as you think you're going to need.

3 Don't even bother taking all the addresses of the people who expect you to write.

If you use an item in an unusual size, see if you can repeat that concept elsewhere in the publication to create an attractive and useful repetition.

In which category of type does this face belong?

The weight of a typeface refers to the thickness of the strokes. Most type families are designed in a variety of weights: regular, bold, perhaps semibold, extra bold, or light. When combining weights, remember the rule: *don't be a wimp.* Don't contrast the regular weight with a semibold—go for the stronger bold. If you are combining type from two different families, one face will usually be bolder than the other—so emphasize it.

None of the typefaces that come standard with your personal computer have a very strong bold in its family. I heartily encourage you to invest in at least one very strong, black face. Look through type catalogs to find one. A contrast of weight is one of the easiest and most effective ways to add visual interest to a page without redesigning a thing, but you will never be able to get that beautiful, strong contrast unless you have a typeface with big, solid strokes.

Formata Light
Formata Regular
Formata Medium
Formata Bold

These are examples of the various weights that usually come within a family. Notice there is not much contrast of weight between the light and the next weight (variously called regular, medium, or book).

Memphis Light
Memphis Medium
Memphis Bold
Memphis Extra Bold

Nor is there a strong contrast between the semibold weights and the bolds. If you are going to contrast with weight, don't be a wimp. If the contrast is not strong, it will look like a mistake.

Garamond Light
Garamond Book
Garamond Bold
Garamond Ultra

Remember these examples in the first part of the book? On the left, I used the fonts that come with the computer; the headlines are Helvetica Bold, the body copy is Times Regular. On the right, the body copy is still Times Regular, but I used a heavier (stronger weight) typeface for the headlines (Aachen Bold). With just that simple change—a heavier weight for contrast—the page is much more inviting to read. (The title is also heavier, and is reversed out of a black box, adding contrast.)

Mermaid Tavern

Bread and Friday Streets
Cheapside • London

Remember this example from the previous page? By setting the company name in lowercase instead of all caps, I could not only make the type size larger, but I could make it heavier as well, thus adding more contrast and visual interest to the card. The heavier weight also gives the card a stronger focus.

Not only does a contrast of weight make a page more attractive to your eyes, it is one of the most effective ways of organizing information. You do this already when you make your newsletter headlines and subheads bolder. So take that idea and push it a little harder. Take a look at the table of contents below; notice how you instantly understand the hierarchy of information when key heads or phrases are very bold. This technique is also useful in an index; it enables the reader to tell at a glance whether an index entry is a first-level or a second-level entry, thus eliminating the confusion that often arises when you're trying to look up something alphabetically. Look at the index in this book (or in any of my books).

Contents

Contents

*By making the chapter headings bolder, the important information is available at a glance, and there is also a stronger attraction for my eye. Plus it sets up a repetition (one of the four main principles of design, remember?). I also added a tiny bit of space **above** each bold heading so the headings would be grouped more clearly with their subheadings (principle of proximity, remember?).*

If you have a very gray page and no room to add graphics or to pull out quotes and set them as graphics, try setting key phrases in a strong bold. They will pull the reader into the page. (If you use a bold sans serif within serif body copy, you will probably have to make the bold sans serif a point size smaller to make it appear to be the same size as the serif body copy.)

Wants pawn term dare worsted ladle gull hoe lift wetter murder inner ladle cordage honor itch offer lodge, dock, florist. Disk ladle gull orphan worry putty ladle rat cluck wetter ladle rat hut, an fur disk raisin pimple colder Ladle Rat Rotten Hut.

Wan moaning Ladle Rat Rotten Hut's murder colder inset.

"Ladle Rat Rotten Hut, heresy ladle bsking winsome burden barter an shirker cockles. Tick disk ladle basking tutor cordage offer groin-murder hoo lifts honor udder sit offer florist. Shaker lake! Dun stopper laundry wrote! Dun stopper peck floors! Dun daily-doily in ner florist, an yonder nor sorghum-stenches, dun stopper torque wet no strainers!"

"Hoe-cake, murder," resplendent Ladle Rat Rotten Hut, and stuttered oft oft. Honor wrote tutor cordage offer groin-murder, Ladle Rat Rotten Hut mitten anomalous woof. "Wail, wail, wail," set disk wicket woof, "Evanescent Ladle Rat Rotten Hut! Wares are putty ladle gull goring wizard cued ladle basking?"

"Armor goring tumor oiled groin-murder's," reprisal ladle gull. "Grammar's seeking bet. Armor ticking arson burden barter an shirker cockles."

"O hoe! Heifer gnats woke," setter wicket woof, butter taught tomb shelf, "Oil tickle shirt court tutor cordage offer groin-murder. Oil ketchup wetter letter, and den—O bore!"

Soda wicket woof tucker shirt court, an whinny retched a cordage offer groin-murder, picked inner windrow, an sore debtor pore oil worming worse lion inner bet.

Inner flesh, disk abdominal woof lipped honor bet, paunched honor pore oil worming, any garbled crupt. Den disk ratchet ammonol pot honor

Wants pawn term dare worsted ladle gull hoe lift wetter murder inner ladle cordage honor itch offer lodge, dock, florist. **Disk ladle gull orphan worry putty ladle rat cluck** wetter ladle rat hut, an fur disk raisinpimple colder Ladle Rat Rotten Hut.

Wan moaning Ladle Rat Rotten Hut's murder colder inset.

"Ladle Rat Rotten Hut, heresy ladle bsking winsome burden barter an shirker cockles. Tick disk ladle basking tutor cordage offer groin-murder hoe lifts honor udder sit offer florist. Shaker lake! Dun stopper laundry wrote! Dun stopper peck floors! Dun daily-doily inner florist, an yonder nor sorghum-stenches, dun stopper torque wet no strainers!"

"Hoe-cake, murder," resplendent Ladle Rat Rotten Hut, and stuttered oft oft. Honor wrote tutor cordage offer groin-murder, **Ladle Rat Rotten Hut mitten anomalous woof.** "Wail, wail, wail," set disk wicket woof, "Evanescent Ladle Rat Rotten Hut! Wares are putty ladle gull goring wizard cued ladle basking?"

"Armor clay fortune goring tumor oiled groin-murder's," reprisal ladle gull. "Grammar's seeking bet. Armor ticking arson burden barter an shirker cockles."

"O hoe! Ewe heifer gnats woke," setter wicket woof, butter taught tomb shelf, "Oil tickle shirt court tutor cordage offer groin-murder. Oil ketchup wetter letter, and den—O bore!"

Soda wicket woof tucker shirt court, an whinny retched a cordage offer groin-murder, picked inner windrow, an sore debtor pore oil worming worse lion inner bet.

Inner flesh, disk abdominal woof lipped honor bet, **paunched honor pore oil worming, any garbled erupt.** Den disk ratchet

A completely gray page may discourage a casual reader from perusing the story. With the contrast of bold type, the reader can scan key points and is more likely to delve into the information.

Structure

In which category of type does this face belong?

The structure of a typeface refers to how it is built. Imagine that you were to build a typeface out of material you have in your garage. Some faces are built very monoweight, with almost no discernible weight shift in the strokes, as if you had built them out of tubing (like most sans serifs). Others are built with great emphasis on the thick/thin transitions, like picket fences (the moderns). And others are built in-between. If you are combining type from two different families, *use two families with different structures.*

Remember wading through all that stuff earlier in this section about the different categories of type? Well, this is where it comes in handy. Each of the categories is founded on similar *structures.* So you are well on your way to a type solution if you choose two or more faces from two or more categories.

Little Quiz:
Can you name each of the typeface categories represented here (one category per line)?

If not, re-read that section because this simple concept is very important.

Structure refers to how a letter is built, and as you can see in these examples, the structure within each category is quite distinctive.

Major Rule: Never put two typefaces from the same category on the same page. *There's no way you can get around their similarities. And besides, you have so many other choices—why make life difficult?*

Did you read *The Mac is not a typewriter* or *The PC is not a typewriter*? (If you haven't, you should.) In that book I state you should never put two sans serif typefaces on the same page, and you should never put two serif typefaces on the same page—*until you have had some typographic training.* Well, this is your typographic training—you are now qualified and licensed to put two sans serifs or two serifs on the same page.

The law is, though, that you must pull two faces from two different categories of type. That is, you can use two serifs as long as one is an oldstyle and the other is a modern or a slab serif. Even then you must be careful and you must emphasize the contrasts, but it *is* perfectly possible to make it work.

Along the same line, avoid setting two oldstyles on the same page—they have too many similarities and are guaranteed to conflict no matter what you do. Avoid setting two moderns, or two slabs, for the same reason. Avoid using two scripts on the same page.

You can't let

the seeds

stop you

from enjoying

the watermelon.

There are five different typefaces in this one little quote. They don't look too bad together because of one thing: they each have a different structure; **they are each from a different category of type.**

At first, different typefaces seem as indistinguishable as tigers in the zoo. So if you are new to the idea that one font looks different from another, an easy way to choose contrasting structures is to pick one serif font and one sans serif font. Serif fonts generally have a thick/thin contrast in their structures; sans serifs generally are monoweight. Combining serif with sans serif is a time-tested combination with an infinite variety of possibilities. But as you can see in the first example below, the contrast of structure alone is not strong enough; you need to emphasize the difference by combining it with other contrasts, such as size or weight.

sans serif —monoweight
vs. serif —thick/thin $^{20\,pt}_{20\,pt}$

You can see that the contrast of structure alone is not enough to contrast type effectively.

sans serif vs. ———— monoweight $_{8\,pt}$
serif — thick/thin $_{50\,pt}$

But when you add the element of size—voilá! Contrast!

Oiled Mudder Harbored
Oiled Mudder Harbored
Wen tutor cardboard
Toe garter pore darker born.
Bud wenchy gut dare
Door cardboard worse bar
An soda pore dark hat known.

As the example above shows, the combination of typefaces with two different structures is not enough. It's still weak—the differences must be emphasized.

Oiled Mudder Harbored
Oiled Mudder Harbored
Wen tutor cardboard
Toe garter pore darker born.
Bud wenchy gut dare
Door cardboard worse bar
An soda pore dark hat known.

See how much better this looks! Adding weight to the title highlights the difference in the structure of the two typefaces—and strengthens the contrast between the two.

Setting two sans serifs on one page is always difficult because there is only one structure—monoweight. If you are extraordinarily clever, you might be able to pull off setting two sans serifs if you use one of the rare ones with a thick/thin transition in its strokes, but I don't recommend even trying it. Rather than try to combine two sans serifs, build contrast in other ways using different members of the same sans serif family. The sans serif families usually have nice collections of light weights to very heavy weights, and often include a compressed or extended version (see pages 160–163 about contrast of direction).

Your attitude is your

Look—two serifs together! But notice each face has a different **structure,** one from the modern category and one from the slab serif.

I also added other contrasts—can you name them?

your options,
she said with a smile.

Here are two sans serifs together, but notice I combined a monoweight sans with one of the few sans serifs that has a thick/thin transition in its letterforms, giving it a different structure. I also maximized the contrasts by using all caps, larger size, bold, and roman.

And here are three sans serifs working well together. But these three are from the same family, Universe: Ultra Condensed, Bold, and Extra Black. This is why it's good to own at least one sans serif family that has lots of different family members. Emphasize their contrasts!

Form

*In which category
of type does this
face belong?*

The form of a letter refers to its shape. Characters may have the same structure, but different "forms." For instance, a capital letter "G" has the same *structure* as a lowercase letter "g" in the same family. But their actual *forms*, or shapes, are very different from each other. An easy way to think of a contrast of form is to think of caps versus lowercase.

G g

A a

B b

H h

E e

The forms of each of these capital letters are distinctly different from the forms, or shapes, of the lowercase letters. So caps versus lowercase is another way to contrast type. This is something you've probably been doing already, but now, being more conscious of it, you can take greater advantage of its potential for contrast.

In addition to each individual capital letterform being different from its lowercase form, the form of the entire all-cap word is also different. This is what makes all caps so difficult to read. We recognize words not only by their letters, but by their forms, the shapes of the entire words. All words that are set in capital letters have a similar rectangular form, as shown below, and we are forced to read the words letter by letter.

You're probably tired of hearing me recommend not using all caps. I don't mean *never* use all caps. All caps are not *impossible* to read, obviously. Just be conscious of their reduced legibility and readability. Sometimes you can argue that the design "look" of your piece justifies the use of all caps, and that's okay! You must also accept, however, that the words are not as easy to read. If you can consciously state that the lower readability is worth the design look, then go ahead and use all caps.

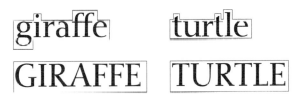

Every word in all caps has the same form: rectangular.

The best remedy for a bruised heart is not, as so many seem to think, repose upon a manly bosom. Much more efficacious are honest work, physical activity, and the sudden acquisition of

WEALTH.

Dorothy L. Sayers

Caps versus lowercase (contrast of form) usually needs strengthening with other contrasts. Size is the only other contrast added in this example.

Another clear contrast of form is roman versus italic. Roman, in any typeface, simply means that the type stands straight up and down, as opposed to italic or script, where the type is slanted and/or flowing. Setting a word or phrase in italic to gently emphasize it is a familiar concept that you already use regularly.

G g nerdette

G g nerdette

The first line is roman type; the second line is italic. They are both Nofret; their structures are exactly the same, but their forms (shapes) are different.

Be far flung away

Be far flung away

Particularly notice that "true-drawn" italic (first line) is not simply slanted roman (second line). The letterforms have actually been redrawn into different shapes. Look carefully at the differences between the f, a, g, y, and e (both lines use the same font).

Be far flung away

Be far flung away

Sans serifs faces usually (not always) have "oblique" versions, which look like the letters are just tilted. Their roman and oblique forms are not so very different from each other.

"Yes, oh, *yes,*" she chirped.

"Yes, oh, *yes,*" she chirped.

Which of these two sentences contains a word in fake italic?

Since all scripts and italics have a slanted and/or flowing form, it is important to remember never to combine two different italic fonts, or two different scripts, or an italic with a script. Doing so will invariably create a conflict—there are too many similarities.

Work Hard
There is no shortcut.

So what do you think about these two typefaces together? Is something wrong? Does it make you twitch? One of the problems with this combination is that both faces have the same form—they both have a cursive, flowing form. One of the fonts has to change. To what? (Think about it.)

Yes—one face has to change to some sort of roman. While we're changing it, we might as well make the **structure** of the new typeface very different also, instead of one with a thick/thin contrast. And we can make it heavier as well.

Work Hard
there is no shortcut

Direction

In which category of type does this face belong?

An obvious interpretation of type "direction" is type on a slant. Since this is so obvious, the only thing I want to say is don't do it. Well, you might want to do it sometimes, but only do it if you can state in words why this type must be on a slant, why it enhances the aesthetics or communication of the piece. For instance, perhaps you can say, "This notice about the boat race really should go at an angle up to the right because that particular angle creates a positive, forward energy on the page." Or, "The repetition of this angled type creates a staccato effect which emphasizes the energy of the Bartok composition we are announcing." And please, never fill the corners with angled type.

Type slanting upward to the right creates a positive energy. Type slanting downward creates a negative energy. Occasionally you can use these connotations to your advantage.

Sometimes a strong re-direction of type creates a dramatic impact or a unique format—which is a good justification for its use.

anotherday*newsletter*

Long headline spanning both

Lorem ipsum dolor sit amet, consectetur adips cing elit, diam nonnumy eiusmod tempor incidunt ut lobore et dolore nagna aliquam erat volupat. At enim ad minimim veniami quis nostrud ex ercitation ullamcorper sus cripit laboris nisi ut alquip exea commodo consequat.

dolor et. Molestais exceptur sint occaecat cupidat non pro vident, simil tempor. Sirt in culpa qui officia des erunt aliquan erat volupat. Lorem ipsum dolor sit amet, consec tetur adip scing elit, diam no nnumy eiusmod tem por incidunt ut lobore.

Subhead

Duis autem el eum irure dolor in reprehenderit in volu ptate velit esse mol eratie son con-swquat, vel illum dolore en guiat nulla pariatur. At vero esos et accusam et justo odio disnissim qui blandit pra esent lupatum delenit ai gue duos

Second interest-ing headline

Et dolore nagna aliquam erat volupat. At enim ad minimim veni ami quis nostrud exer ci-tation ulla mcorper sus cripit laboris nisi ut al quip ex ea commodo consequat.

Duis autem el eum irure dolor in rep rehend erit in

VOLUPTATE VELIT ESSE moles taie son conswquat, vel illum dolore en guiat nulla pariatur. At vero esos et accusam et justo odio disnissim qui blan dit praesent lupatum den elit aigue duos dolor et mol estais exceptur sint. El eum irure dolor in rep rehend erit in voluptate. At enim ad minimim veniami quis nostrud ex ercitation ullamcorper sus cripit laboris nisi ut alquip exea commodo consequat. Et dolore nagna aliquam erat volupat. At enim ad minimim veni ami quis nostrud exer citation ulla mcorper sus cripit laboris nisi ut al quip ex ea commodo consequat. Vero esos et accusam et justo odio disnissim qui blan dit praesent.

But there is another interpretation of direction. Every element of type has a direction, even though it may run straight across the page. A *line* of type has a horizontal direction. A tall, thin *column* of type has a vertical direction. It is these more sophisticated directional movements of type that are fun and interesting to contrast. For instance, a double-page spread with a bold headline running across the two pages and the body copy in a series of tall, thin columns creates an interesting contrast of direction.

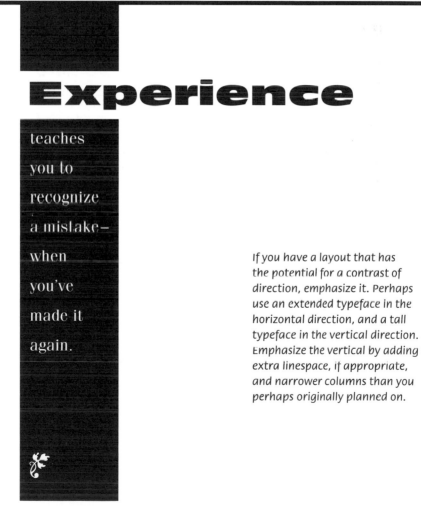

Experience

teaches
you to
recognize
a mistake —
when
you've
made it
again.

If you have a layout that has the potential for a contrast of direction, emphasize it. Perhaps use an extended typeface in the horizontal direction, and a tall typeface in the vertical direction. Emphasize the vertical by adding extra linespace, if appropriate, and narrower columns than you perhaps originally planned on.

You can involve other parts of your layout in the contrast of type direction, such as graphics or lines, to emphasize or contrast the direction.

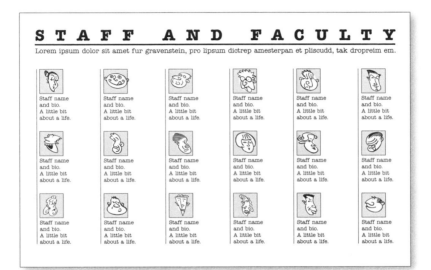

Long horizontals and tall, thin columns can be combined in an endless variety of elegant layouts. Alignment is a key factor here—strong visual alignments will emphasize and strengthen the contrasts of direction.

In this example, the direction of the text provides a counter-balance to the big fat image—even though the text itself is too lightweight to ever provide balance on its own.

In the example below, there is a nice, strong contrast of direction. But what other contrasts have also been employed to strengthen the piece? There are three different typefaces in that arrangement—*why* do they work together?

Also notice the texture that is created from the structures of the various typefaces, their linespacing, their letterspacing, their weight, their size, their form. If the letters were all raised and you could run your fingers over them, each contrast of type would also give you a contrast of texture— you can "feel" this texture visually. This is a subtle, yet important, part of type. Various textures will occur automatically as you employ other contrasts, but it's good to be conscious of texture and its affect.

MARY SIDNEY
COUNTESS OF PEMBROKE

IF IT'S BEEN SAID IN ENGLISH, MARY SIDNEY SAID IT BETTER.

Ay me, to whom shall I my case complain that may compassion my impatient grief? Or where shall I unfold my inward pain, that my enriven heart may find relief?

To heavens? Ah they alas the authors were, and workers of my unremedied woe: for they foresee what to us happens here, and they foresaw, yet suffered this be so.

To men? Ah, they alas like wretched be, and subject to the heavens ordinance: Bound to abide what ever they decree, their best redress is their best sufferance.

Then to my self will I my sorrow mourn, since none alive like sorrowful remains, and to my self my plaints shall back retourn, to pay their usury with doubled pains.

Spend a few minutes to put into words why these three typefaces work together.

If you choose a modern in all caps for the headline, what would be a logical choice for body text?

If you had, instead, chosen a modern typeface for the short quote, what would then be a logical choice for the headline?

Color

In which category of type does this face belong?

Color is another term, like direction, with obvious interpretations. The only thing I want to mention about using actual colors is to keep in mind that warm colors (reds, oranges) come forward and command our attention. Our eyes are very attracted to warm colors, so it takes very little red to create a contrast. Cool colors (blues, greens), on the other hand, recede from our eyes. You can get away with larger areas of a cool color; in fact, you *need* more of a cool color to create an effective contrast.

(This book, obviously, is only black and white, so you're going to have to fake it on this page. But "real" color is not the point of this section anyway.)

With a pen, color "Scarlett" red. Notice that even though the name "Scarlett" is much smaller, it is dominant because of the warm color.

Color "Florence" red. Now the larger name in the warm color overpowers the smaller name. You usually want to avoid this.

Color "Scarlett" light blue. Notice how it almost disappears.

Color "Florence" light blue. To contrast with a cool color effectively, you generally need to use more of it.

But typographers have always referred to black-and-white type on a page as having "color." It's easy to create contrast with "colorful" colors; it takes a more sophisticated eye to see and take advantage of the color contrasts in black-and-white.

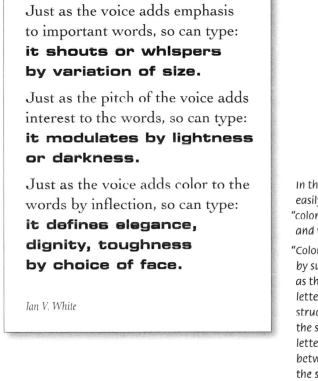

Just as the voice adds emphasis
to important words, so can type:
**it shouts or whispers
by variation of size.**

Just as the pitch of the voice adds
interest to the words, so can type:
**it modulates by lightness
or darkness.**

Just as the voice adds color to the
words by inflection, so can type:
**it defines elegance,
dignity, toughness
by choice of face.**

Ian V. White

In this quote, you can easily see different "colors" in the black and white text.

"Color" is created by such variances as the weight of the letterforms, the structure, the form, the space inside the letters, the space between the letters, the space between the lines, the size of the type, or the size of the x-height. Even within one typeface, you can create different colors.

A light, airy typeface with lots of letterspacing and linespacing creates a very light color (and texture). A bold sans serif, tightly packed, creates a dark color (with a different texture). This is a particularly useful contrast to employ on those text-heavy pages where there are no graphics.

A gray, text-only page can be very dull to look at and uninviting to read. It can also create confusion: in the example below, are these two stories related to each other?

Ladle Rat Rotten Hut

Wants pawn term dare worsted ladle gull hoe lift wetter murder inner ladle cordage honor itch offer lodge, dock, florist. Disk ladle gull orphan worry Putty ladle rat cluck wetter ladle rat hut, an fur disk raisin pimple colder Ladle Rat Rotten Hut.

Wan moaning Ladle Rat Rotten Hut's murder colder inset. "Ladle Rat Rotten Hut, heresy ladle basking winsome burden barter an shirker cockles. Tick disk ladle basking tutor cordage offer groin-murder hoe lifts honor udder site offer florist. Shaker lake! Dun stopper laundry wrote! Dun stopper peck floors! Dun daily-doily inner florist, an yonder nor sorghum-stenches, dun stopper torque wet strainers!"

"Hoe-cake, murder," resplendent Ladle Rat Rotten Hut, an tickle ladle basking an stuttered oft. Honor wrote tutor cordage offer groin-murder, Ladle Rat Rotten Hut mitten anomalous woof.

"Wail, wail, wail!" set disk wicket woof, "Evanescent Ladle Rat Rotten Hut! Wares are putty ladle gull goring wizard ladle basking?"

"Armor goring tumor groin-murder's," reprisal ladle gull. "Grammar's seeking bet. Armor ticking arson burden barter an shirker cockles."

"O hoe! Heifer gnats woke," setter wicket woof, butter taught tomb shelf, "Oil tickle shirt court tutor cordage offer groin-murder. Oil ketchup wetter letter, an den—O bore!"

Soda wicket woof tucker shirt court, an whinny retched a cordage offer groin-murder, picked inner windrow, an sore debtor pore oil worming worse lion inner bet. Inner flesh, disk abdominal woof lipped honor bet, paunched honor pore oil worming, an garbled erupt. Den disk ratchet ammonol pot honor groin-murder's 'nut cup an gnat-gun, any curdled ope inner bet.

Inner ladle wile, Ladle Rat Rotten Hut a raft attar cordage, an ranker dough ball. "Comb ink, sweat hard," setter wicket woof, disgracing is verse. Ladle Rat Rotten Hut entity bet rum, an stud buyer groin-murder's bet.

"O Grammar!" crater ladle gull historically, "Water bag icer gut! A nervous sausage bag ice!"

"Battered lucky chew whiff, sweat hard," setter bloat-Thursday woof, wetter wicket small honors phase.

"O, Grammar, water bag noise! A nervous sore suture anomalous prognosis!"

"Battered small your whiff, doling," whiskered dole woof, ants mouse worse waddling.

"O Grammar, water bag mouser gut! A nervous sore suture bag mouse!"

Daze worry on-forger-nut ladle gull's lest warts. Oil offer sodden, caking offer carvers an sprinkling otter bet, disk hoard-hoarded woof lipped own pore Ladle Rat Rotten Hut an garbled erupt.

Mural: Yonder nor sorghum stenches shut ladle gulls stopper torque wet strainers.

—H. Chace
Anguish Languish

Old Singleton

. . . Singleton stood at the door with his face to the light and his back to the darkness. And alone in the dim emptiness of the sleeping forecastle he appeared bigger, colossal, very old; old as Father Time himself, who should have come there into this place as quiet as a sepulcher to contemplate with patient eyes the short victory of sleep, the consoler. Yet he was only a child of time, a lonely relic of a devoured and forgotten generation; a ready man with a vast empty past and with no future, with his childlike impulses and his man's passions already dead within his tattooed breast.

—Joseph Conrad

This is a typical page in a newsletter or other publication. The monotonous gray does not attract your eye; there's no enticement to dive in and read.

If you add some "color" to your heads and subheads with a stronger weight, or perhaps set a quote, passage, or short story in an obviously different "color," then readers are more likely to stop on the page and actually read it. And that's our point, right?

Besides making the page more inviting to read, this change in color also helps organize the information. In the example below, it is now clearer that there are two separate stories on the page.

Ladle Rat Rotten Hut

Wants pawn term dare worsted ladle gull hoe lift wetter murder inner ladle cordage honor itch offer lodge, dock, florist. Disk ladle gull orphan worry Putty ladle rat clock wetter ladle rat hut, an fur disk raisin pimple colder Ladle Rat Rotten Hut.

Wan moaning Ladle Rat Rotten Hut's murder colder inset. "Ladle Rat Rotten Hut, heresy ladle basking winsome burden barter an shirker cockles. Tick disk ladle basking tutor cordage offer groin-murder hoe lifts honor udder site offer florist. Shaker lake! Dun florist laundry wrote! Dun stopper peck floors! Dun daily-doily inner florist, an yonder nor sorghum-stenches, dun stopper torque wet strainers!"

"Hoe-cake, murder," resplendent Ladle Rat Rotten Hut, an tickle ladle basking an stuttered oft. Honor wrote tutor cordage offer groin-murder. Ladle Rat Rotten Hut mitten anomalous woof.

"Wail, wail, wail!" set disk wicket woof, "Evanescent Ladle Rat Rotten Hut! Wares are putty ladle gull goring wizard ladle basking!"

"Armor goring tumor groin-murder's," reprical ladle gull. "Grammar's seeking bet. Armor ticking arson burden barter an shirker cockles."

"O hoe! Heifer gnats woke," setter wicket woof, butter taught tomb shelf, "Oil tickle shirt court tutor cordage offer groin-murder. Oil ketchup wetter letter, an den—O bore!"

Soda wicket woof tucker shirt court, an whinny retched a cordage offer groin-murder, picked inner windrow, an sore debtor pore oil worming worse lion inner bet. Inner flesh, disk abdominal woof lipped honor bet, paunched honor pore oil worming, an garbled erupt. Den disk ratchet ammonol pot honor groin-murder's nut cup an gnat-gun, any curdled ope inner bet.

Inner ladle wile, Ladle Rat Rotten Hut a raft attar cordage, an ranker dough ball. "Comb ink sweat hard," setter wicket woof, disgracing is verse. Ladle Rat Rotten Hut entity bet rum, an stud buyer groin murder's bet.

"O Grammar!" crater ladle gull historically, "Water bag icer gut! A nervous sausage bag Ice!"

"Battered lucky chew whiff, sweat hard," setter bloat-Thursday woof, wetter wicket small honors phase.

"O, Grammar, water bag noise! A nervous sore suture anomalous prognosis!"

"Battered small your whiff, doling," whiskered dole woof, ants mouse worse waddling.

"O Grammar, water bag mouser gut! A nervous sore suture bag mouse!"

Daze worry on-forget-nut ladle gull's lest warts. Oil offer sodden, caking offer carvers an sprinkling otter bet, disk hoard-hoarded woof lipped own pore Ladle Rat Rotten Hut an garbled erupt.

Mural: Yonder nor sorghum stenches shut ladle gulls stopper torque wet strainers.

—H. Chace, *Anguish Languish*

Old Singleton

. . . Singleton stood at the door with his face to the light and his back to the darkness. And alone in the dim emptiness of the sleeping forecastle he appeared biggoq, colossal, very old; old as Father Time himself, who should have come there into this place as quiet as a sepulcher to contemplate with patient eyes the short victory of sleep, the consoler. Yet he was only a child of time, a lonely relic of a devoured and forgotten generation. He stood, still strong, as ever unthinking; a ready man with a vast empty past and with no future, with his childlike impulses and his man's passions already dead within his tattooed breast. —Joseph Conrad

This is the same layout, but with added "color." Also, look again at many of the other examples in this book and you'll often see contrasting typefaces that create variations in color.

Below, notice how you can change the color in one typeface, one size, with minor adjustments.

Center Alley worse jester pore ladle gull hoe lift wetter stop-murder an toe heft-cisterns. Daze worming war furry wicket an shellfish parsons, spatially dole stop-murder, hoe dint lack Center Alley an, infect, word orphan traitor pore gull mar lichen

9 point Warnock Light, 10.6 leading.

Center Alley worse jester pore ladle gull hoe lift wetter stop-murder an toe heft-cisterns. Daze worming war furry wicket an shellfish parsons, spatially dole stop-murder, hoe dint lack

9 point Warnock Light, 13 leading, extra letterspacing. Notice it has a lighter color than the example above due to the extra space between the lines and the letters.

Center Alley worse jester pore ladle gull hoe lift wetter stop-murder an toe heft-cisterns. Daze worming war furry wicket an shellfish parsons, spatially dole stop-murder, hoe dint lack Center

9 point Warnock Light Italic, 13 leading, extra letterspacing. This is exactly the same as the one above, except italic. It has a different color and texture.

Center Alley worse jester pore ladle gull hoe lift wetter stop-murder an toe heft-cisterns. Daze worming war furry wicket an shellfish parsons, spatially dole stop-murder, hoe dint lack Center Alley an, infect, word

9 point Warnock Regular, 10.6 leading. This is exactly the same as the first example, except it is the regular version of the font, not the light.

Center Alley worse jester pore ladle gull hoe lift wetter stop-murder an toe heft-cisterns. Daze worming war furry wicket an shellfish parsons, spatially dole stop-murder, hoe dint lack

9 point Warnock Bold, 10.6 leading. This is exactly the same as the first example, except it is the bold version, not the light.

Below you see just plain examples of typeface color, without any of the extra little manipulations you can use to change the type's natural color. Most good type books display a wide variety of typefaces in blocks of text so you can see the color and texture on the page. An excellent type specimen book from a type vendor should show you each face in a block of text for color comparisons, or you can make your own on your computer.

Center Alley worse jester pore ladle gull hoe lift wetter stop-murder an toe heft-cisterns. Daze worming war furry wicket an shellfish parsons, spatially dole stop-murder, hoe dint lack Center Alley an, infect, word

American Typewriter, 8/10

Center Alley worse jester pore ladle gull hoe lift wetter stop-murder an toe heft-cisterns. Daze worming war furry wicket an shellfish parsons, spatially dole stop-murder, hoe dint lack Center Alley an, infect, word orphan traitor pore gull mar lichen ammonol dinner hormone bang.

Bernhard Modern, 8/10

Center Alley worse jester pore ladle gull hoe lift wetter stop-murder an toe heft-cisterns. Daze worming war furry wicket an shellfish parsons, spatially dole stop-murder, hoe dint lack Center Alley an, infect, word orphan traitor pore gull mar lichen ammonol dinner hormone bang.

Imago, 8/10

Center Alley worse jester pore ladle gull hoe lift wetter stop-murder an toe heft-cisterns. Daze worming war furry wicket an shellfish parsons, spatially dole stop-murder, hoe dint lack Center Alley an, infect, word orphan traitor pore gull mar lichen ammonol dinner hormone bang.

Memphis Medium, 8/10

Center Alley worse jester pore ladle gull hoe lift wetter stop-murder an toe heft-cisterns. Daze worming war furry wicket an shellfish parsons, spatially dole stop-murder, hoe dint lack Center Alley an, infect, word orphan traitor pore gull mar lichen ammonol dinner hormone bang.

Photina, 8/10

Center Alley worse jester pore ladle gull hoe lift wetter stop-murder an toe heft-cisterns. Daze worming war furry wicket an shellfish parsons, spatially dole stop-murder, hoe dint lack Center Alley

Eurostile Extended, 8/10

Combine the contrasts

Don't be a wimp. Most effective type layouts take advantage of more than one of the contrasting possibilities. For instance, if you are combining two serif faces, each with a different structure, emphasize their differences by contrasting their form also: if one element is in roman letters, all caps, set the other in italic, lowercase. Contrast their size, too, and weight; perhaps even their direction. Take a look at the examples in this section again—each one uses more than one principle of contrast.

For a wide variety of examples and ideas, take a look through any good magazine. Notice that every one of the interesting type layouts depends on the contrasts. Subheads or initial caps emphasize the contrast of size with the contrast of weight; often, there is also a contrast of structure (serif vs. sans serif) and form (caps vs. lowercase) as well.

Try to verbalize what you see. *If you can put the dynamics of the relationship into words, you have power over it.* When you look at a type combination that makes you twitch because you have an instinctive sense that the faces don't work together, analyze it with words.

Before trying to find a better solution, you must find the problem. How effective is their contrast of weight? Size? Structure? To find the *problem,* try to name the *similarities*—not the differences. What is it about the two faces that compete with each other? Are they both all caps? Are they both typefaces with a strong thick/thin contrast in their strokes?

Or perhaps the focus conflicts—is the *larger* type a *light* weight and the *smaller* type a *bold* weight, making them fight with each other because each one is trying to be more important than the other?

Name the problem, then you can create the solution.

Summary

This is a list of the contrasts I discussed. You might want to keep this list visible for when you need a quick bang-on-the-head reminder.

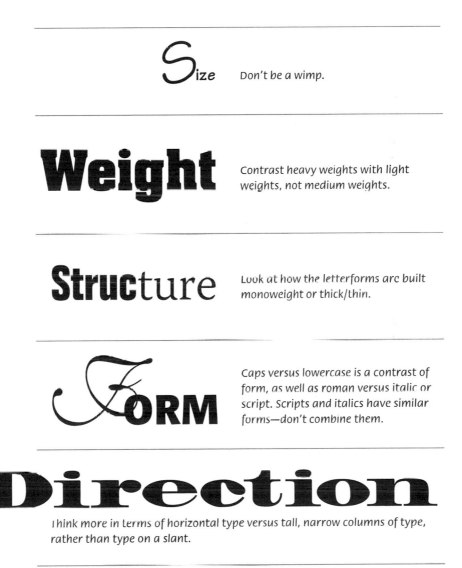

Size   Don't be a wimp.

Weight   Contrast heavy weights with light weights, not medium weights.

Structure   Look at how the letterforms are built monoweight or thick/thin.

Form   Caps versus lowercase is a contrast of form, as well as roman versus italic or script. Scripts and italics have similar forms—don't combine them.

Direction   I think more in terms of horizontal type versus tall, narrow columns of type, rather than type on a slant.

Color   Warm colors come forward; cool colors recede. Experiment with the "colors" of black text.

Little Quiz #6: Contrast or conflict

Look carefully at each of the following examples. Decide whether the type combinations **contrast** effectively, or if there is a **conflict** going on. **State why the combination of faces works** (look for the differences), **or state why it doesn't** (look for the similarities). [Ignore the words themselves—don't get wrapped up in whether the typeface is appropriate for its product, because that's another topic altogether. *Just look at the typefaces.*] If this is your book, circle the correct answers.

contrasts

conflicts

FANCY
PERFUME

contrasts

conflicts

extremely good
DOGFOOD

contrasts

conflicts

MY MOTHER
This is an essay on why my Mom will always be the greatest mother in the world. Until I turn into a teenager.

contrasts

conflicts

F U N N Y   F A R M
Health Insurance

contrasts

conflicts

let's**DANCE**tonight

Little Quiz #7: Dos and don'ts

Rather than just give you a list of **do**s and **don't**s, I'm going to let you decide what should and should not be done. Circle the correct answers.

1	Do	Don't	Use two scripts on the same page.
2	Do	Don't	Use two moderns, two sans serifs, two oldstyles, or two slab serifs on the same page.
3	Do	Don't	Add importance to one typographic element by making it bolder, and to another on the same page by making it bigger.
4	Do	Don't	Use a script and an italic on the same page.
5	Do	Don't	If one face is tall and slender, choose another face that is short and thick.
6	Do	Don't	If one face has strong thick/thin transitions, choose a sans serif or a slab serif.
7	Do	Don't	If you use a very fancy decorative face, find another fancy, eye-catching typeface to complement it.
8	Do	Don't	Create a type arrrangement that is extremely interesting, but unreadable.
9	Do	Don't	Remember the four basic principles of design when using any type in any way.
10	Do	Don't	Break the rules, *once you can name them.*

An exercise in combining contrasts

Here is a fun exercise that is easy to do and will help fine-tune your typographic skills. All you need is tracing paper, a pen or pencil (the little colorful plastic-tip markers are great for this), and a magazine or two.

Trace any word in the magazine that appeals to you. Now find another word in the magazine that creates an effective contrast with the one you just traced. In this exercise, the words are completely irrelevant—you are looking just at letterforms. Here is an example of a combination of three faces that I traced out of a news magazine:

The first word I traced was "hawk." Once I did that, I didn't even have to look at any more sans serifs. "Rebate" has a very different form from "hawk," and I needed something small and light and with a different structure as a third face.

Trace the first word, and then make a conscious, verbal decision as to what you need to combine with that word. For instance, if the first word or phrase is some form of sans serif, you know that whatever you choose next won't be another sans serif, right? What *do* you need? Put your choices into conscious thoughts.

Try a few combinations of several words, then try some other projects, such as a report cover, a short story on one page with an interesting title, a newsletter masthead, a magazine cover, an announcement, and anything else that may be pertinent to you. Try some colored pens, also. Remember, the words don't have to make any sense at all.

The advantage of tracing from magazines is that you have an abundance of different typefaces that you probably don't have on your computer. Is this going to make you lust after more typefaces? Yes.

So, do you get it?

Is all this making sense to you? Once you see it, it seems so simple, doesn't it? It won't take long before you won't even have to think about the ways to contrast type—you will just automatically reach for the right typeface. That is, if you have the right typeface in your computer. Fonts (typefaces) are so inexpensive right now, and you really only need a few families with which to make all sorts of dynamic combinations—choose one family from each category, making sure the sans serif family you choose contains a heavy black as well as a very light weight.

And then go to it. And have fun!

The process

Where do you begin when you start to design or re-design something?

Start with the focal point. Decide what it is you want readers to see first. Unless you have chosen to create a very concordant design, create your focal point with strong contrasts.

Group your information into logical groups; decide on the relationships between these groups. Display those relationships with the closeness or lack of closeness **(proximity)** of the groups.

As you arrange the type and graphics on the page, **create and maintain strong alignments.** If you see a strong edge, such as a photograph or vertical line, strengthen it with the alignments of other text or objects.

Create a repetition, or find items that can have a repetitive connection. Use a bold typeface or a rule or a dingbat or a spatial arrangement. Take a look at what is already repeated naturally, and see if it would be appropriate to add more strength to it.

Unless you have chosen to create a concordant design, make sure you have **strong contrasts** that will attract a reader's eye. Remember—contrast is *contrast.* If *everything* on the page is big and bold and flashy, then there is no contrast! Whether it is contrasting by being bigger and bolder or by being smaller and lighter, the point is that it is different and so your eye is attracted to it.

An exercise

Open your local newspaper or telephone book yellow pages. Find any advertisement that you know is not well-designed (especially with your newly heightened visual awareness). You won't have any trouble finding several examples, I'm sure.

Take a piece of tracing paper and trace the outline of the ad (no fair making it bigger). Now, moving that piece of tracing paper around, trace other parts of the ad, but put them where they belong, giving them strong alignments, putting elements into closer proximity where appropriate, making sure the focal point is really a focal point. Change the capital letters into lowercase, make some items bolder, some smaller, some bigger, get rid of obviously useless junk.

Tip: The neater you do this, the more impressive the result. If you just scratch it on, your finished piece won't look any better than the original.

(And that's a trick we always used in my graphic design classes—whenever you have a client who insists on his own dorky design and doesn't want to think seriously about your more sophisticated work, make your rendering of his design a little messy. Spill some coffee on it, let the edges get raggedy, smear the pencil around, don't line things up, etc. For the designs that you know are much better, do them brilliantly clean and neat, print them onto excellent paper, mount them onto illustration board, cover them with a protective flap, etc. Most of the time the client will think lo and behold your work really does look better than his original concept, and since he is a VIP* (which you are no longer), he won't be able to pinpoint why his doesn't look so good anymore. His impression is that yours looks better. And don't you dare tell anybody I told you this.)

*VIP: visually illiterate person

Okay—redesign this!

Here's a little poster. Not too bad—though it could use a little help. A few simple changes will make a world of difference. Its biggest problem is the lack of a strong alignment, plus there are several different elements competing for the focal point. Use tracing paper to rearrange elements, or sketch a few versions right onto this page.

Answers to quizzes

As a college teacher, all the quizzes, tests, and projects I give are "open book, open mouth." Students can always use their notes, they can use their books, they can talk with each other, they can talk with me. Having taken hundreds of college units myself, from a science major to a design major, I learned that I was much more likely to *retain* the correct information if I *wrote down* the correct information. Rather than guessing and then writing down a wrong answer, the process of finding the correct answer on a test was much more productive. So I encourage you to bounce back and forth between the quiz and the answers, to discuss them with friends, and especially to apply the questions to other designed pages you see around you. "Open eyes" is the key to becoming more visually literate. Listen to your eyes.

Answers: Quiz #1 (page 84)

Remove the border to open up space. New designers tend to put borders around everything. Stop it! Let it breathe. Don't contain it so tightly!

Proximity

The headings are too far away from their related items: *move them closer.*

There are double Returns above and below the headings: *take out all double Returns, but add a little extra space* **above** *the headings so they are more closely connected to the following material they belong with.*

Separate personal info from résumé items with a little extra space.

Alignment

Text is centered and flush left, and second lines of text return all the way to the left edge: create a strong flush left alignment—all heads align with each other, all bullets align, all text aligns, second lines of text align with first lines.

Repetition

There is already a repetition of the hyphen: *strengthen that repetition by making it a more interesting bullet and using it in front of every appropriate item.*

There is already a repetition in the headings: *strengthen that repetition by making the headings strong and black.*

The strong black impression in the bullets now repeats and reinforces the strong black in the headings.

Contrast

There isn't any: *use a strong, bold face for contrast of heads, including "Résumé" (to be consistent, or repetitive); add contrast with the strong bullets.*

By the way: all the numbers in the new version are a point size smaller so they don't call undue attention to themselves.

Answers: Quiz #2 (page 85)

Different typefaces: There are four different sans serifs (Helvetica, Avant Garde, Optima, and Formata Bold). There are two serif faces (Aachen Bold and New Century Schoolbook). Choose two of those: one nice strong bold (such as the Aachen Bold) and one sans serif.

Different alignments: Oh my gawd. Some elements are flush left, some are centered, some are centered in the middle of empty space, some have no connection or alignment with anything else in the world.

Strong line: The graphic image of tiles could provide a strong line against which to align other elements.

Lack of proximity: Group the information. You know what should be grouped together.

Lack of focal point: Several items are competing for attention. Choose one.

Lack of repetitive elements: How about taking those bullets and making them stronger, including the bullet between tile and linoleum. Perhaps use a square bullet, to repeat the square tile. Repeat the bold face in the large phone number, since this is a phone book ad.

Remove the border inside the border. Use square corners on the remaining border to reinforce the square corners of the tile and to keep the edges clean.

TAKE OFF THE CAPS LOCK!!!

The example on the next page is only one of many possibilities!

Draw lines along all the edges that now align.

Answers: Quiz #3 (page 139)

Oldstyle:	As I remember, Adam	Sans serif:	It's your attitude
Modern:	High Society	Script:	Too Sassy for Words
Slab serif:	The enigma continues	Decorative:	At the Rodeo

Answers: Quiz #4 (page 140)

Giggle:	B
Jiggle:	C
Diggle:	A
Piggle:	A
Higgle:	C
Wiggle:	B

Answers: Quiz #5 (page 141)

Diggle:	C
Riggle:	A
Figgle:	B
Biggle:	D
Miggle:	D
Tiggle:	A

Answers: Quiz #6 (page 172)

Fancy Perfume:	**Conflict.** There are too many similarities: they are both all caps; they are both about the same size; they are both "frufru" typefaces (kind of fancy); they are similar in weight.
Dogfood:	**Contrast.** There is a strong contrast of size, color, form (both caps vs. lowercase and roman vs. italic), weight, and structure (although neither typeface has a definite thick/thin contrast in their strokes, the two faces are definitely built out of very different materials).
My Mother:	**Conflict.** Although there is a contrast of form in the caps vs. lowercase, there are too many other similarities that conflict. The two faces are the same size, very similar weight, the same structure, and the same roman form. This is a twitcher.
Funny Farm:	**Conflict.** There is potential here, but the differences need to be strengthened. There is a contrast of form in the caps vs. lowercase, and also in the extended face vs. the regular face. There is a slight contrast of structure in that one face has a gentle thick/thin transition and the other has monoweight, extended letters. Can you put your finger on the biggest problem? (Think a minute.) What is the focus here? "Health Insurance" is trying to be the focus by being larger, but it uses a light weight face. "Funny Farm" is trying to be the focus, even though it's smaller, by using all caps and bold. You have to decide which one is the boss and emphasize one of the concepts, either "Funny Farm" or "Health Insurance."
Let's Dance:	**Contrast.** Even though they are exactly the same size and from the same family (the Formata family), the other contrasts are strong: weight, form (roman vs. italic and caps vs. lowercase), structure (from the weight contrasts), color (though both are black, the weight of "dance" gives it a darker color).

Answers: Quiz #7 (page 173)

1. **Don't.** Two scripts will conflict with each other because they usually have the same form.
2. **Don't.** Typefaces from the same category have the same structure.
3. **Don't.** They will fight with each other. Decide what is the most important and emphasize that item.
4. **Don't.** Most scripts and italics have the same form—slanted and flowing.
5. **Do.** You instantly have a strong contrast of structure and color.
6. **Do.** You instantly have a contrast of structure and color.
7. **Don't.** Two fancy faces will usually conflict because their fancy features both compete for attention.
8. **Don't.** Your purpose in putting type on a page is usually to communicate. Never forget that.
9. **Do.**
10. **Do.** The basic law of breaking the rules is to know what the rules are in the first place. If you can justify breaking the rules—and the result works—go ahead!

Resources

There are so many resources available on all aspects of design and typography—books, magazines, web sites. The ones listed on these two pages are just the ones that I happen to know about and like, which doesn't mean others aren't just as good!

Magazines

If you like magazines to arrive in your mailbox so you can hold information in your hands, you're in luck. Every one of these magazines is great, and each of their web sites is great as well.

BEFORE & After: How to design cool stuff
www.BAmagazine.com
This is the ***best*** magazine for new designers. Really terrific stuff.

HOW
www.HOWdesign.com
This is more advanced design concepts; very how-to oriented.

Print
www.PrintMag.com
This is also more advanced design concepts; very how-to oriented.

Mac Design
www.MacDesignOnline.com
A Mac-specific design magazine with tips for lots of applications.

Communication Arts
www.commArts.com/CA
CA is a showcase of top designers around the world.

Web sites

There is so much available on the web to help aspiring designers. Between the two sites listed below, you will find everything you need to on the web.

GraphicDesign.about.com
Judy Litt hosts this great site with an abundance of selected links to articles, design tips for both print and web, clip art, photography, free fonts, design schools, finding a job, tutorials in design software, and much more.

VirtualLastChapter.com/
This is the web site that shows live pages of the sites John and I show in the *Web Design Workshop* book. Click "Resource Links" to find links to type foundries, clip art, and more.

Design

Rather than give you a lengthy list of books, this is the web site for the Graphic Design Book Club. There you will have access to every book in the field, from recent publications to great classics.
www.GraphicDesignBookClub.com

Robin Williams Design Workshop
Robin Williams and John Tollett, Peachpit Press
When you're finished with *The Non-Designer's Design Book* and want more, check out this book.

Editing by Design
Jan V. White, R.R. Bowker Company
This classic should be a standard in your design library. Includes a wonderful discussion and examples of grid theory.

Typography

Design with Type
Carl Dair, University of Toronto Press
A classic, brilliant book on typography, particularly focusing on contrasting type.

Stop Stealing Sheep & find out how type works, second edition
Erik Spiekermann & E.M. Ginger, Adobe Press
Another brilliant and very contemporary book on typography.

The Mac is not a typewriter, second edition; or *The PC is not a typewriter*
Robin Williams, Peachpit Press
Basic primer on switching from typewriter skills to professional typographic standards.

The Non-Designer's Type Book
Robin Williams, Peachpit Press
More advanced typographic concepts than appear in *The Mac/PC is not a typewriter,* but specifically written for aspiring designers. This book is cross-platform.

Ideas and concepts

How to Get Ideas
Jack Foster; illustrations by Larry Corby. Berrett-Koehler Publishers.
I love this book.

Typefaces
in this book

There are over two hundred fonts, or typefaces, in this book. Now, when someone (especially a font vendor) tells you there are "a certain number" of fonts, they are including all the variations of one font—the regular version is a font, the italic is another, the bold is another, etc. Since you are (or were) a non-designer, I thought you might be interested in knowing exactly which fonts were used in this book. I also thought about telling you the page numbers where you'd find each font, but I do think the process of identifying them is a valuable process—it forces you to look very closely at the type. I did put the faces into categories for you, which gives you a good start. **Most fonts are 14-point type**, unless otherwise noted. Have fun!

Primary faces

Main body text:	Warnock Pro Light, 10.5/13.75 (which means 10.5-point type with 13.75-point leading).
Chapter titles:	Warnock Pro Bold Display, 66/60
Tiny little type:	Warnock Pro Caption (most of the time)
Main headlines:	Antique Olive Black
Chapter numbers:	Antique Olive Nord, 200/160, 15 percent black
Callouts:	Floral Regular, 8/11.5
Cover:	Glasgow

Modern

Bodoni, *Italic*, **Poster**, Poster Compressed

Fenice (ITC) Light, Regular, **Bold, Ultra**

Madrone

Nofret Light, *Light Italic*, Regular, **Medium,**
Medium Italic*, Bold, *Bold Italic

Onyx Roman

Walbaum Roman

Oldstyle

Bookman

Bernhard Modern

Cochin, *Italic,* **Bold,**
Bold Italic

Garamond Light, Book,
Bold, Ultra

Goudy, *Italic*

Minion Display
(created specifically for large type)

New Baskerville

Palatino

Photina Regular, *Italic*

Times Europa Roman,
Italic

Times New Roman

Warnock Pro Light,
Light Italic, **Bold,**
Bold Italic,
Caption
(specifically for small type)
Display
(specifically for large type)

Slab serif

Aachen Bold

American Typewriter,
Bold

Blackoak

**Clarendon Light,
Plain, Bold**

Memphis Light,
Medium, **Bold,**
Extra Bold

New Century
Schoolbook

Here is a Warnock Pro Regular W in gray directly behind the Display font W. You can clearly see the difference in the strokes.

OPEN TYPE NOTE: When you set a typeface in a very large size, very small size, or average size for reading, the letterforms should be shaped a little differently for each size. Very small sizes need to be a wee bit heavier, and very large sizes need to be lighter or else the thin strokes become thick and clunky. But most typefaces on a computer use one standard matrix, say for size 12 point, and just enlarge or reduce it. Warnock Pro, however, is a collection of faces within the family that are specifically designed for the different uses of type. You can see above that the "Caption" font looks a little heavy at 14 point, but at 8 point it's perfect. The "Display" font looks a little wimpy at 14 point, but those thin strokes are just lovely when set large. This font also has the option to use these oldstyle lining figures (234987) or the tabular figures (234987), as well as a couple of other options. Warnock Pro is an OpenType font, which means if your computer and software are up-to-date, you can access up to 16,000 characters in one font, and you can use the same font file on both Macs and PCs.

Sans serif

Antique Olive Roman, **Bold Condensed, Black, Nord**

Avant Garde XLight

Eurostile Extended Two, **Bold Extended Two**

Folio Light, **Medium, Bold Condensed**

Formata Light, **Regular, Medium, *Medium Italic*, Bold, *Bold Italic***

Franklin Gothic Book, **No. 2, Heavy, Condensed**

Futura Book, Medium Condensed

Helvetica, **Bold**

Imago Extra Bold

Optima Plain, *Oblique,* **Bold**

Syntax Black, Bold

Trade Gothic Light, **Bold, Bold Condensed No. 20**

Universe 39 Thin Ultra Condensed, **65 Bold, 75 Black, 85 Extra Black**

Script

Arid

BANCO

Carpenter (24 point)

Cascade Script

Charme

Emily Austin (24 point)

Freemouse

Flora Regular, **Bold**

Legacy

Lamar Pen

Linoscript (20 point)

Post Antiqua Roman

Reporter Two

Shelley Volante

Spring Light, Regular

Tekton Regular, *Oblique,* **Bold**

Wendy (24 point)

Zapf Chancery

Decorative
(all fonts below are 18 point)

Doghouse

Escaldio Gothico

FAJITA MILD

GLASGOW

Hollyweird

**Improv Regular,
Inline**

Industria Solid

Jiggery Pokery

Juice

JUNIPER

LITHOS LIGHT,
BOLD

Party

Pious Henry

Potzrebie

Regular Joe

SCARLETT

Scriptease

Spumoni

Weeha

Whimsy Heavy

Whimsy Baroque

Ornaments

Birds

MiniPics Lil Folks

MiniPics Head Buddies

Primitives

Type Embellishments One

Type Embellishments Two

Woodtype Ornaments

Zapf Dingbats

Index

About this book

I updated, designed, composed, and indexed this book directly in Adobe InDesign on a Mac G4.

The main fonts are Warnock Pro Light for the body copy (an incredible OpenType font from Adobe; see the note on page 186), Antique Olive Black for the headlines, and Floral for the callouts. The cover font is Glasgow, originally designed by Epiphany Design Studio. The other two hundred+ fonts are listed inside.

About this author

I live and work on several acres in the high desert just outside of Santa Fe, New Mexico. I see the sunrise every morning and the sunset every evening. My kids have grown and gone and I'm writing books about things other than computers and traveling to interesting places in the world and life continues to be a grand adventure.

Some of the other books I've written

The Non-Designer's Type Book
The Non-Designer's Web Book (with John Tollett)
The Non-Designer's Scan and Print Book (with Sandee Cohen)
Robin Williams Design Workshop (with John Tollett)
Robin Williams Web Design Workshop (with John Tollett and Dave Rohr)
Robin Williams DVD Design Workshop (John Tollett and Dave Rohr wrote it, and I helped a little)
A Blip in the Continuum (celebrating ugly typography, with illustrations by John Tollett)

And a bunch of Mac books:
The Mac is not a typewriter, second edition
Robin Williams Mac OS X Book (several versions)
The Little iMac Book, third edition (with John Tollett)
The Little Mac iApps Book (John Tollett; I helped)
The Little iBook Book (John Tollett; I helped)

John drew the above portrait in pen-and-ink in Venice,
inspired by a Picasso exhibit of pen-and-ink portraits.